"Our purpose and strategy are now crisper, clearer and more focused."

KERSTYN COMLEY, CO-CEO OF MEETOO EDUCATION LTD

CREATING STRATEGY

A PRACTICAL GUIDE

MICHAEL BERNARD

Creating Strategy

First published in 2021 by

Panoma Press Ltd
48 St Vincent Drive, St Albans, Herts, AL1 5SJ, UK
info@panomapress.com
www.panomapress.com

Book layout by Neil Coe.

978-1-784529-61-1

To my wife Catherine and children Christopher,
Henry and Dominic with my daughter-in-law Mary,
who together provide my purpose!

TESTIMONIALS

"Michael has helped us to completely transform the way that we think about our mission, our strategy and our values. Our purpose and strategy are now crisper, clearer and more focused. It has reinvigorated the whole organisation."

Kerstyn Comley, Co-CEO of MeeToo Education Ltd

"Michael's structure and coaching really helped us distil our broad direction into a coherent strategy. The structure has turned out to be durable, and we are still using it to positive effect today. Once created, a decent strategy offers a framework which simplifies operational decision-making. Recommended!"

Gary Moore, CEO of AbilityNet

"Michael's help in creating our strategy has been invaluable. His communication, both written and spoken, is notable for its complete absence of jargon, conveying complex ideas with simple and compelling clarity. You always feel you are making progress and get a sense of satisfaction as the pieces click into place.

His book is a must-have for anyone who wants their strategy to live and inspire."

Andrew Hobbs, Head of Downside School

"As a business owner of a successful publishing and events company, I found my discussions with Michael illuminating and very rewarding. He has a very clear understanding of all the components which build company strategy and how and why these need to be carefully defined. There is no one in my experience who has conceptualised this better. As a company which has grown rapidly over the past decade or so and wants to keep on developing, Michael's precise insights into strategy were enormously helpful in formulating my own thinking in wanting to put theory into practice. I can't wait to read Michael's book because I know it will be invaluable."

Mark Allen, Chairman of Mark Allen Group

"An absolute must-read for anyone involved in the development of strategy for their organisation. A practical, down to earth guide using case studies to illustrate what happens when strategies are well developed and when they are not!"

Janet Morris, Non-Executive Director, Trustee and Consultant

ACKNOWLEDGEMENTS

First of all, I have to recognise that almost everything I have learned about business and strategy was through my work for IBM over more than 30 years. It's a very different company to the one I joined in 1981, but still an extraordinary one filled with hugely talented people.

As I then worked with other organisations, I would like to thank those at AbilityNet (a charity that provides technological support to those with impairments), The Royal Humane Society (a charity that recognises life-saving and bravery); Downside school; Exeter Business School and in particular its outstanding MBA course; MeeToo Help (a social enterprise providing help to young people with mental health concerns) and last, but not least, Southern Health NHS Foundation Trust. It has been my role to provide guidance and challenge to these organisations, but I have found that I have been challenged just as much by them to keep learning and broadening my thinking.

To many friends, colleagues and contributors, a profound thank you: Martin Beckwith, Janet Morris, Chris Barraclough, Andrew Chapman, Alan Barnard, Martin Thomas, Mark Allen, Brendan Dineen, Mike Lusby and many others, including those who contributed case studies that had to be anonymised. If you should be on this list and are not, I apologise for my faulty memory!

CONTENTS

INTRODUCTION

"Strategy is everything."

Sergio Zyman (former CMO of Coca Cola)

When I took up my first board role, I had to learn a new set of skills. Instead of being responsible for day-to-day activities, as I was in my day job, my new role was to ensure that the executive team ran the organisation effectively. As I have taken on additional such roles, one of the most frequent tasks has been to review strategy work and make sure that it is done well. Every board should believe that it is responsible for the strategy of the organisation that it serves. This is one of the most important roles of a board.

The way this usually works, in theory, is that 1-2 weeks before the board meeting, papers are sent out so that the board can read them, come to the meeting without needing to have the paper presented from scratch, and then a useful discussion can take place. In practice, papers are often sent out at the last minute or even not sent in advance at all.

Oddly, given that presenting strategies to the board is done so regularly, the quality of strategy has been uniformly weak. The reasons are usually very similar and drove me to think about why people don't write better strategies.

It seems to me there are two fundamental problems. The first is that most people who write strategies have very little training, coaching or experience in doing so. The second is that those who review them don't know what to look for or how to assess the quality of what they are looking at. Given how important it is for any organisation to have a good strategy, there's little to no training available on how to create one. Even an MBA course will not give much practice in writing strategies, even if they spend quite a lot of time looking at case studies and critiquing them. In my experience, companies don't send employees on courses about strategy. They don't expect people to read books on strategy as part of their development plans. There isn't a formal career path that leads to chief strategy officer unless it is working for a consultancy and then going client-side. There isn't – to my knowledge – a professional body for strategy writers. So I suppose it's not very surprising that many of the people who do the task lack the necessary skills.

While consultants can help with a structure and process for creating strategy and by providing input, particularly in the analysis stage, the key decisions have to be taken within the company. These are some of the most important bets that the leadership team will make, and it is inconceivable to me that outsourcing responsibility for strategic decisions is consistent with good leadership or good governance.

The purpose of this book is, therefore, to give a relatively simple guide to anyone writing a strategy paper for an organisation, large or small. It's based on my experience in IBM, a leading business school, a social enterprise, charities and the NHS, on my own learnings from trying to write them myself, with varying levels of success, and on many conversations I've had as I researched and discussed this topic.

When I started my first marketing job at IBM in 1994, one of the first things that my boss asked me to do was to write a marketing strategy for the product we were responsible for in the UK. I look back with horror at the voluminous document that ended up being produced with 'help' from an internal consultant. Eighty-something pages, if I recall correctly, filled from top to bottom with data, graphs and portentous management speak. It didn't help anyone (except, indirectly, me – by getting my first taste of dissatisfaction at the investment of time and effort for no return) and was quietly consigned to a cupboard to languish in peace and do no further harm. Over the years, I had many more attempts and was able to inspect and learn from other peoples' strategies, including those of clients and business partners. Eventually, I was responsible for some years for writing the marketing strategy for IBM UK and was one of a team of four writing the overall company strategy for the UK and Ireland.

More recently, as I have worked on boards as a non-executive director, trustee, governor and advisor, I have had the chance to look at and review many strategies for organisations and parts of organisations. In many cases, the same mistakes crop up again and again, most of them very basic. What I have found, in general, is that the longer the strategy paper, the less likely it is to lay out a case for change. In some cases, papers are a long and convoluted plea to be left alone to get on with what is already being done – which is the antithesis of what a strategy should be.

Writing a strategy is both a science and an art. Whatever you do, it's got to be a useful document. In an attempt to demystify the process, I explain at a high level some of the terms that frequently crop up in companies and other bodies when people write strategies. Understand the key terms, but don't be intimidated by them.

The main points to remember are that your strategy should be an important – indeed, essential – document, and it needs to be used and acted on. Otherwise, everyone is wasting their time. All too often, a strategy is written to justify what is already happening rather than as a vital exercise to determine what to change.

As with so many things in business, there's no single right answer for any part of this, and it should never turn into a box-ticking project. A scientific approach is a good start, but thinking is an art, and art is famously resistant to rigid rules. However, there are good practices to follow.

I have tried to avoid hard prescriptions and proscriptions throughout, as I have found myself to be wrong so often in the past that it seems sensible to allow for exceptions to what are general 'rules'.

My experience also tells me that there are some fairly basic principles that have a good chance of getting you on the right path. I strongly suggest you start with the recommended approach – at least until you find it does not deliver what you need.

Throughout the book, there are a number of case studies – some from well-known international companies and some from smaller organisations. I have interviewed a number of people who have kindly contributed case studies. Some are great examples of strategic work; others are illustrations of what happens when it's done badly. In some of the latter examples, I have anonymised the organisation and the contributor for obvious reasons. I am therefore obliged to omit these contributors from the list of people to thank. You know who you are and how grateful I am for the time you spent discussing these situations. Having said that, even if the company's identity is concealed, each story is as accurate as I could make it, and I have attempted to bring out the key learnings despite the obligation to hide some details.

When decisions are written up in case studies, no one wants to admit that their bold masterstroke was just a lucky guess, so it turns into a great strategic decision. While there are plenty of case studies throughout this book, please be aware of their limitations.

There is a real temptation when working on strategy to look for a 'formula' or a set of templates to complete which will deliver a strategy. What I have seen is that this makes it much harder to do the most important thing when creating strategy, which is to *think*. By all means, use tools to help you do this work – and I will discuss several later – but remember that like all tools, they are to make a task easier or faster, and their use is not in itself the answer. That's why you will not find any templates in this book.

Is this book for you? If your full-time day job is writing the strategy for a multi-national organisation, then I really hope that you don't need to read this book – although if you do, you may find some insights that are helpful. I have had a very specific individual in mind when putting this together: an executive in a medium-size organisation who is responsible for a significant number of people, a reasonable budget, and who has risen to their executive role through a good level of professional skills and appropriate experience, but who has not had any training on writing a strategy. This individual has probably written one or more strategies for their function but has found it a difficult and somewhat dispiriting task. This book is for you – and I hope you get a lot out of it.

In the end, if you aren't fascinated and convinced by the strategy you are writing, why would you expect anyone else to be?

Michael Bernard

July 2021

Note: the use of the word 'company' throughout this book does not necessarily imply a commercial organisation. The point being made will apply equally to a government or 3rd sector organisation unless specifically excluded.

EXECUTIVE SUMMARY

"Plan for what is difficult while it is still easy;
do what is great while it is still small."

**Sun Tzu (Chinese general, military strategist,
writer and philosopher)**

Here is a summary of this book which, owing to the format, spills onto a second page.

- A strategy is an organisational plan to:
  - respond to the current or expected situation or
  - meet one or more goals, and
  - which requires collaborative effort and a complex response.

- Most strategies are not written well, are not reviewed and are never fully executed.

- Strategies are written in response to a situation – opportunity or problem – or to meet specific goals.

- A strategy needs firm foundations. These come from having a clear purpose, mission and vision.

- Every strategy must have goals, either as the start point for the strategy or to clearly lay out what it will do to meet the situation. These goals must be SMART.

- A strategy consists of three elements: strategic analysis, strategic intent and strategic actions.

- A strategy is all about selecting priorities and managing time, money and people to deliver the goals.

- A strategy has to be about change, as no organisation exists in a static world. The speed of change required is at least the speed of external change; otherwise, the strategy is a path to failure, whether slow or fast.

- What medium you use and what style you use are less important than having something concise and easy to understand.

- Once the strategy is approved, communicate it to all stakeholders, especially employees, and then make it a central part of everything you do.

- Keep it updated and fresh. Measure results, adapt and update the strategy in line with performance and circumstances, but never lose sight of what you are trying to achieve.

CHAPTER 1:

What is a Strategy, and Why Is One Needed?

"Strategy is a style of thinking, a conscious and deliberate process, an intensive implementation system, the science of insuring future success."

Pete Johnson (Strategic planning & execution specialist)

"The essence of strategy is choosing what not to do."

Michael Porter (Academic, business author, advisor and speaker)

"Success is 20% skills and 80% strategy. You might know how to succeed, but more importantly, what's your plan to succeed?"

Jim Rohn (Entrepreneur, author and motivational speaker)

Creating a strategy is difficult and hard work. If it were easy, then there would be no need for the dozens of books on the subject, and the strategies brought forward for approval would be high quality and successful. Even harder is getting a well-crafted strategy executed.

If you are going to spend some time reading a book about how to write a strategy, it would be good to have a definition of what the word means. Like so many things in life, the more closely one looks at this, the harder it is to pin down. While the origins of the word strategy come from a military background, it is so widely used nowadays that it has almost lost a clear meaning. How often have you heard someone saying, "We need a strategy" or "This needs a strategic approach" about a trivial issue? If someone is a 'strategic thinker', what do we mean?

If you look up the definition of strategy on Wikipedia, it tells you the following:

"Strategy (from the Greek στρατηγία stratēgia, "art of troop leader; office of general, command, generalship") is a high-level plan to achieve one or more goals under conditions of uncertainty."

Trying to define what a strategy is seems to me like trying to grasp a bar of wet soap. Just when you think you have a grip on it, it slips out. I'll have a go at defining the meaning shortly because I think having a definition is more helpful than not, but I am sure there will be all kinds of exceptions to any definition. I was confident that strategy was at least a response to a longer-term situation – many months if not several years – but then recalled that Formula 1 teams have a race strategy for every time they are out on the circuit. That is the purest example I can think of showing the execution of a complete and complex strategy over a two-hour period. So I've had to craft a definition that doesn't exclude Mercedes, Red Bull, Ferrari and others from consideration. This would be an unusual

– perhaps unique, until somebody tells me otherwise – case where creating the strategy takes longer than its execution. See the Formula 1 case study for more insights.

What is a strategy for? Everywhere I look tells me that it is about gaining sustainable competitive advantage, increasing revenue and/or profits or meeting customer needs better. These thoughts are not helpful if you are not a commercial organisation. The Department of Defence doesn't have profits or customers, so does that mean they don't need a strategy? Similarly, unless you are the US or China, your defence strategy is not going to be about gaining a competitive advantage, sustainable or not.

It isn't even about having a plan to keep the organisation alive; as a charity whose purpose is the eradication of, for example, polio, will have a strategy to make itself redundant – for good reason. No, the point of having a strategy is to fulfil the purpose of the organisation. In the next chapter, we will look at purpose, among other terms. For now, think about your strategy as a plan intended to bring the organisation closer to the vision it holds.

Broadly, there are two situations that demand a strategy or strategic response, situational and goal-based. There is a third reason that strategies are created: when they are required by an external body, such as inspectors or regulators. This, of course, is a terrible reason to create strategy, but it does happen.

1. Situational

A situational strategy is one that is dictated by the external circumstances of the organisation. A company may find that it is suddenly disrupted by a new entrant to a previously predictable market. A government body may be required to work to radically revised budgets or respond to a new regulatory regime. A charity may need to respond to changes in the tax treatment of donations.

A far-sighted leader may not wait for an external stimulus and create a strategy based on insight into the organisation, the environment in which it operates and what changes will be needed. The best leaders formulate a strategy that disrupts the market and changes the game. However, much as we all like to read the case studies about IKEA and Apple, there aren't many times when the readers of this book will be able to build those kinds of strategies, and so we will keep our feet on the ground.

The situational strategy is much beloved by authors and consultants. We see big, bold examples of companies operating at a global level; we see charismatic leaders making good – and sometimes bad – choices, and we see case studies of companies that succeed in style (Apple, General Electric, Google and many others). In practice, most situational strategies are written because there is a major opportunity, a significant problem, or a crisis. You don't have to be a 'visionary leader' to spot a good opportunity opening up, but you do have to know a great deal about your market, customers, clients or users and the strengths and weaknesses of your own organisation. Responding to a crisis is not usually a matter of choice or knowledge. Opportunity and crisis are related: those organisations that spot opportunities early and exploit them will cause the crisis for slower-moving companies. External crises that affect everyone, such as the Covid-19 emergency that we face as I write, are hard – by definition – to spot and plan for. If this were not the case, we would all be better prepared.

Let's look at an example of a situational strategy.

When Toyota started importing cars into the US in the 1960s, their rapid growth – along with other Japanese manufacturers – began to cause problems for them as the US car manufacturers were finding it difficult to compete and lobbied hard for protection. For many years, the US government discussed voluntary limits on imports. Clearly, Toyota could not continue on a path of manufacturing in their home country and exporting to the US, as this risked a hard limit on sales and exposed their manufacturing investment to significant risk.

Therefore, Toyota pursued a strategy of local production in the US. They explored a joint venture with Ford, but this never got off the ground. A joint venture (JV) with General Motors did, however, see the light of day. They formed New United Motor Manufacturing, Inc. (NUMMI), the JV to last for a maximum of 12 years, with 50:50 investment and intention to manufacture 200,000 units a year at GM's recently closed Fremont plant in California which would be re-opened.

This was also a big risk – and a big bet – by Toyota. Recruiting in the same talent pool as local manufacturers, having to work with the same union restrictions, and dealing with the same cultural issues of attitudes to work all might be thought to limit their capabilities, on the grounds that they would suffer from the same problems as GM. However, Toyota's competitive advantage in lean manufacturing persisted in the US market. By expanding local production, the release of new models suited to the US market, and the development of its sales network, they saw a significant increase in sales. Between 1998 and 2004, Toyota's sales rose from 900,000 units to 2.06 million, growing further still to 2.62 million vehicles in 2007. The company's market share also rose – from 6.1 per cent in 1988, passing 10 per cent in 2001, and growing to 16.1 per cent in 2007.[1]

By setting a strategy of local production, counting on their ability to manufacture better and cheaper than the US competition, they were able to operate in the same environment, with access to the same labour force, and achieve better results. As Michael Porter put it in his seminal book on competitive strategy: "Competitive strategy involves positioning a business to maximise the capabilities that distinguish it from its competitors." Toyota made their big bet on being able to implement better manufacturing practices than local companies could – and their bet paid off.

2. Goal-oriented

In the commercial world, the goals can be decided by the board, and therefore become secondary to a situational strategy. However, for mature businesses quoted on the stock markets, there is huge pressure to deliver – quarter by quarter – to the expectations of their shareholders. The better established an organisation, the more it is constrained to deliver what it has forecast to Wall Street. At the very least, this provides one very important parameter for any strategy, and in the worst case, the strategy may be built entirely around stock market-based goals.

In the world of private equity owned businesses, the pressure to deliver to specific numbers within tight timescales can be even stronger.

At a lower level, any large organisation will have divisions, functions and possibly areas that it needs to succeed.

- Division: a part of the organisation tasked with a specific mission. General Electric, for example, has divisions for Aviation, Power, Renewable Energy, Healthcare, Additives, Digital, Research and others. Each one of these will need a strategy to meet the expectations (goals) of the parent company.

- Function: a large organisation will recognise that some key functions are common to all divisions and areas. These would include Finance, HR, Sales, Marketing, Operations etc. In many organisations, there will be a Group Head of these functions who will produce a strategy to (re-)define the outputs and outcomes provided, as well as how to recruit, train, develop, retain, motivate and reward those working in this function.

- Area: a large organisation may have distinct operations in different parts of the world: US and Canada; EMEA; AP; South America etc. Areas may refer to different parts of one country: England, Northern Ireland, Wales and Scotland within the UK, for example, or even specific counties with the UK. Each will need a strategy to match local market conditions while meeting group targets or goals.

These internal structures will almost certainly be given goals to achieve by the parent organisation. While the goals may well be subject to negotiation, once finalised, they must be met. Usually, there will be three or five-year goals to be met, which leads us straight to the need for a strategy.

Case study: IBM

I don't think IBM needs much introduction, but for those not familiar with the company, it's one of the major vendors in the IT world, with offerings covering Cloud, AI, Analytics, Security, Hardware, Consulting, Outsourcing etc.

In 2010, IBM was looking happily at the progress it had made in improving its earnings per share (EPS) from $6.05 in 2006 to $10-11 by the end of 2010. Management had done well – mostly recompensed in share options; they watched the stock price rise from $81 in January 2006 to $147 by the end of December 2010.

This looked like a great way to make money – for investors as well as the leadership of the company. So, the decision was taken to repeat the exercise, only this time, the EPS target would be set to $20 within five years.

The fundamental problem with the strategy is that it was based on a single financial measure, EPS. If there is one thing that never seems to work in the long run, it is setting one such goal because it misses the whole purpose of the organisation.

The consequence of such a strategy was that it became a list of sub-objectives related to EPS (productivity, increased revenue, acquisitions) with no connection with clients, business partners, employees, suppliers or communities. As each segment of the plan was executed and failed to deliver the improvements expected, the only response left was to cut costs and keep buying back shares. Buying back shares – all other things being equal – means that the EPS increases as the number of shares decreases. If one loses sight of the company purpose, this can appear like a good way to satisfy the shareholders, but in reality, it's an illusion. No extra value is really being created.

For a while, momentum carried things forward. After a while, though, it became clear that the desired result was not only unachievable, it was having negative impacts throughout the company. By 2014, *Business Week* was pointing out that, "IBM's soaring earnings per share and its share price are built on a foundation of declining revenues, capability-crippling offshoring, fading technical competence, sagging staff morale, debt-financed share buybacks, non-standard accounting practices, tax-reduction gadgets, a debt-equity ratio of around 174 per cent, a broken business model and a flawed forward strategy."[2]

By October 2014, the new CEO, Ginni Rometty, had to announce the abandonment of the roadmap, and shortly afterwards, the CFO, who was the architect of the plan, left the company. The legacy of this strategy was 22 consecutive quarters of revenue decline, a sequence only broken in the 4th quarter of 2017.

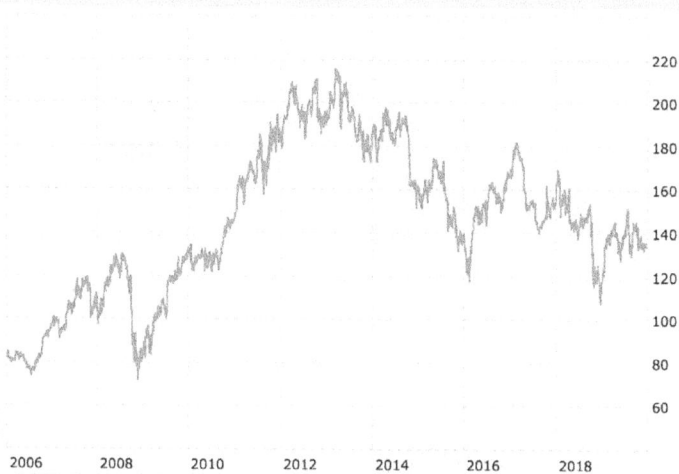

Figure 1. IBM share price history from early 2006 to Jan 2020. Source: Macrotrends.com. Reproduced with permission.

Note the sharp rise during the period of 'success' of the EPS strategy between 2006 and mid-2013 (with a sharp dip during the financial crisis of 2008) and then the decline from nearly $220/share to $110 in 2018, with a recovery around the time of the announcement of the acquisition of Red Hat, in October 2018.

Learnings:

As we will see in the chapter on goals, setting a single goal – especially a financial one – is a very poor approach. Having a set of headlines with no real plan to achieve it was clearly a problem. Phrases such as 'move to high-growth segments' were no more than intentions (good or otherwise). In the end, a financial wish-list, no matter how authoritatively presented, is not a strategy. The strategy had very little connection with externalities; it looked like everything was within IBM's control – which of course, it wasn't.

The result of such a strategy was a broader impact on the capabilities of the company caused by a lack of focus on what ought to have been equally important strategic goals. A specific EPS target can be entirely appropriate if part of a broader strategy that, for example, sets goals on customer net promoter scores, new client wins, employee engagement and so on.

The vast majority of strategies have some kind of goal(s) set by leaders or stakeholders. Even for large companies, the expectations of Wall Street or the London Stock Exchange are hard to ignore. Strategies will be – to a greater or lesser extent – premised on the revenue, profit and EPS expectations of investors.

Strategy vs planning

Creating a strategy is a *part* of planning. Planning is to think about the future of your organisation and to decide what changes are needed to maintain or create the outcomes you want.

- Planning can be for the very short-term: agile stand-ups, for example, are about deciding what work needs to be done today; or for the very long-term: China's President Xi has set the modernisation goal of China becoming a fully developed nation by 2049.[1]

- Planning ultimately results in a set of actions to be executed. In most cases, these actions are to be performed by people working at many different levels in the organisation, which means that the plans have to be translated into work instructions.

Whether the type of strategy is situational or goal-oriented, there has to be a way to judge success. Either type will have one or more goals. The former will set goals that match the organisation's response to the situation, and the latter will derive a strategy from the goals that have been set. Either way, you cannot have a strategy without goals. I can't stress this point enough.

I have seen a lot of so-called strategies with no declared goals or goals so ambiguously defined that it is impossible to know when they have been met (a smart move if you want to declare success on paper – but of no use to really help an organisation). See the discussion of goals in Chapter 3.

Even with a few examples, we can see some themes emerging:

- It's a type of **plan.**
- It addresses a complex situation (war, industry, politics etc.).
- There are goals to be achieved.
- It's not an easy thing to do.
- It involves bringing together resources to achieve the goals.
- It usually takes considerable time to define and implement the strategy and deliver the goals.

For the purposes of this book, I will work to the following definition:

A strategy is an organisational plan to:

- *respond to the current or expected situation or*
- *meet one or more goals, and*
- *which requires collaborative effort and a complex response.*

Business author Pearl Zhu echoes this view: "A strategy is multi-dimensional planning, multi-team collaboration, and multitasking action."

Operational planning, in contrast, is about what everyone does each time they come to work. Metrics are collected and examined frequently, process improvement is key, and much operational improvement is now performed through agile teams.

Let's take a look at a business that is literally very fast-moving, to see an unusual example of strategy:

Case Study: Formula 1

Perhaps the most unusual example of a strategy that will be covered in this book is the Formula 1 race strategy. It's unusual because the strategy takes longer to create than it does to execute, because the entire period of execution is about two hours, and because it is extraordinarily data-rich and scientific.

However, it does conform to my definition of a strategy :

A strategy is an organisational plan to

- *respond to the current or expected situation or*
- *meet one or more goals, and*
- *which requires collaborative effort and a complex response.*

The race strategy is there to get the best place possible at the end of the race. For some teams, this may be first place; for others, their best outcome is a podium place, and for many, it's simply to score some points. This is a great example of a goal-based strategy. The goal could hardly be clearer.

I have been lucky enough to spend some time with a Formula 1 team at their headquarters, and what strikes one is the sheer size of organisation needed to place two cars on the grid. There are perhaps 700 employees dedicated to nothing else, a huge site with seven or eight large buildings and an air of total professionalism. When you are greeted by the receptionist, a cover is placed over your phone camera to ensure there is no accidental loss of important information.

The heart of the building on race weekends is the theatre-style operations centre, where the race is monitored remotely. While some of the support team are present at the track, there are many more who are working in the operations centre during practice, qualifying and the race itself. This is an industry that is incredibly data-rich. There are more than 300 sensors on a car, and during the two-hour race, something like 750 million pieces of data will be transmitted to the team.[3] Over a race weekend, as much as 300GB of data may be transmitted from the car, including the driver's biometrics such as pulse rate and blood pressure. Other types of data will include speed, exhaust and tyre temperatures, clutch fluid pressure, oil and water levels, engine RPM and G-force.

Of course, all that data is analysed in real-time and also after the race to learn about the performance of the car and the thousands of components. That information forms the basis for starting the next race strategy.

What is considered in the strategy? There are many factors to be considered: fuel load, tyre wear, how difficult it is to overtake on any given track, traffic, weather forecasts, the length of the pit lane, likelihood of the safety car, quality of the driver, constantly changing situation on the track, along with a host of other factors. The teams are forbidden to encrypt communication between driver and pit so that each team can listen to the conversations taking place with rival teams. Because of changes to race rules, weather conditions, tyre characteristics, driver skills and experience, the strategy will change each year for the same track.

An F1 race strategy then is just as difficult to work out as any other. The main difference is that it is created 21 times a year and uses very different techniques. But the three key components (which I cover in much more detail in later chapters) are all there:

1. Strategic analysis – possibly the most thorough strategic analysis that I am aware of, with millions of pieces of data considered, including the history of the team's performance on that track, the performance of rival teams (and expectations of how that will change if they are introducing new features for their car), driver performance, weather forecasts etc. Even what would seem to be a very ordinary item – the weather forecast – can become a source of competitive advantage if the precision (how small an area can have a forecast) and accuracy (does the predicted weather occur) can be improved. The team will use complex computer models and game theory to arrive at the likelihood of specific outcomes. For example, they might suggest that a wet race with a two-stop strategy will deliver a 30% chance of a podium place.

2. Strategic intent – the team will go for a three-stop strategy, for example. There's our simple strategic intent based on their highly detailed strategic analysis.

3. Strategic actions – some possible examples:

- Start on soft compound tyres.
- Start with a light load of fuel.
- Pit early and change to harder tyres for a long stint.
- Second and third pit stops will switch to soft compound tyres for a sprint to the finish.

Of course, as with all good strategies, there will be assessments of the assumptions, risks and dependencies. There will be a plan for what to do if the weather unexpectedly deteriorates, if there is a crash and the pace car is deployed, and so on.

A contact at a well-known Formula 1 race team told me:

"Tyre selection has to happen 14 weeks before the race (if it's a race where we have to fly the cars and team), which means the team are already thinking about car performance and how they will run the race, particularly pit stops, months before we actually show up to the race.

We are also second-guessing what the competition might be doing. To a point where you might even opt for a backup race strategy at this stage, knowing that's the best chance of doing something different to your direct rivals.

We've seen a lot of games recently from teams with lodging complaints about other teams. This is mostly strategic. The detail of the complaint, the timing, are all carefully planned to exact the most disruption on the rival team and also extract the most information and insights from the results of the complaint. Right now, all teams will be making strategic decisions that will not materialise until 2022 about car development under the new sets of regulations: what type of car architecture and overall set up and so on."

Of course, as my contact mentions, F1 teams have other strategies. There will be a season-long strategy based on what they can afford to do, sponsorship opportunities, expected technical developments, the balance of effort on developing the current car versus next year's, and so on. I would expect them also to have a business strategy that looks several seasons out. For some teams with financial difficulties, their room for action may be very limited. It's a tough sport. I felt very privileged to be able to get a small glimpse into their world.

Learnings:

Strategies may be found in places and in situations that are unexpected; this doesn't mean they aren't strategies. The characteristics of a strategy remain consistent and are not arbitrarily varied. In such a competitive environment, it is easy to see why a great strategy is required. Most organisations outside this sport are in exactly the same need of good strategic thinking, but their slower pace can allow people to take their eye off the strategic ball. Lastly, an organisation can have need of several different types of strategy. In this case, there's a business strategy, a race season strategy and 21 separate strategies, one for each race.

The relationship between the organisation and strategy

This, as we will see from various case studies, is a complex area. One case study (BHWG) didn't define a formal strategy at all – at least until they were bought by a larger agency. Other, larger organisations require a much more formal planning process. The larger the organisation, the more likely it is to need a strategy that is written down and widely disseminated. The problem comes – just as it does in the day-to-day management of a large and complicated company – when you try to reconcile the requirements of different parts of the organisation.

In a conversation with a friend of mine who is the global CMO of a financial services company, we talked about their model for very loose control from the centre. Most of the international companies under their umbrella view themselves as autonomous businesses, and direction from the top can be rejected without much (if any) internal political risk. How, he mused, should one go about creating a global strategy for this kind of company?

We didn't have time to get into the detail and come up with an answer, but my own thinking was that there was no point building a strategy that depended on the usual command and control. Instead, it had to be about building a global brand that provided such benefits to the local businesses that they were willing – indeed enthusiastic – to bind themselves to that branding and the contingent practices that gave consistency to the brand experience. This could ultimately convince them that closer integration would be more of a benefit than a hindrance.

A **strategy cycle** is the time needed to prepare, create or revise, review and approve all strategies within an organisation. The strategy cycle has to leave time to get execution underway so that results can feed back into the next cycle. If you don't get this right, you will have part of the organisation still working on the strategy when you start the next cycle, and you have lost touch either with the real world on one hand, or the ability to influence strategy lower down in the company on the other.

Let's consider a theoretical example of a large multinational organisation. The first assumption is that the overall company strategy has to come first. It appears obvious that this should be the case so that the overall strategy can be consistently understood and included in planning by all parts of the organisation. Even a company that is purely a holding company for a number of unrelated organisations may find value not only in having a strategy (I would expect, of course, that it does) but also in making that strategy clear to the subsidiary companies. They may benefit in their planning from understanding the criteria (for example) for making further acquisitions and disposing of parts of the portfolio. This may make them very sensitive to the overall needs of the parent company, even if the strategy of the subsidiary would have no other link.

Back to our multinational: each part of the organisation can start building the strategy once they have an outline from the part above it in the hierarchy. It does not have to wait for the final approved version, but there will be a lag. In our theoretical company:

- Worldwide strategy work starts at the beginning of April and is shared in a preliminary version at the start of July. It receives board final approval by the end of September.

- EMEA strategy work starts in July and is shared with countries at the start of August. It receives formal approval from the worldwide team at the end of October.

- Country strategy is built between August and the end of November, when it receives formal approval, giving one month to prepare for implementation on the 1st of January.

So, eight months of the cycle are needed before the strategy approved by the worldwide board becomes the approved strategy at the country level. This is not to say that operational changes can't be made much faster. But that's the point – if you just want to have one simple strategy that is executed under one point of central control, you probably work in a fairly small and autocratic organisation. A larger organisation needs a strategy for each unit that reflects the different nature of their market (EMEA is not the same as Asia Pacific, for example), division or function.

Now let's layer in some more real-world complexity. While the EMEA strategy referred to here is being built, so are the divisional strategies. Imagine you have a division for Industrial Products. How does the Industrial Products worldwide strategy influence the EMEA strategy, which has to deal with not just Industrial Products, but also Retail Products, Custom Products, the Service and Maintenance Division and the Consulting Division? It's not easy, and the intersections are where your problems and opportunities usually arise.

Last but not least, if your organisation is truly customer-first, then it is the 'lowest' level of the company that is closest to the customer, and that has the best understanding of what works and what doesn't work in their patch; what the real competitive situation is; what trends are emerging; what complaints are coming in; and what the workforce is really thinking. So how do you include all these elements in the overall strategy?

As you will have realised, there are not going to be any easy answers to how this can be optimised. However, there are a few principles that can help if observed.

- Encourage collaboration. In this example, the EMEA strategy team should be talking to and working with the global divisions. Yes, this makes it more complicated, but a small amount of collaborative work upfront can save much effort later by avoiding mutually incompatible – or even competitive – plans. This also gives an opportunity to find areas of mutual focus and thus make the most effective use of investments, as well as making strategy sign-off simpler and quicker.

- Think about how the strategy cycle is designed. Instead of a full annual cycle, consider a full cycle every two, or even three, years. Hold a strategy review and update in the other year(s) but cut the cycle time to one month. Of course, changing circumstances may make this difficult, but it could save a lot of time and effort.

- Involve people from all layers of the organisation in the strategy work. If you get those who spend a lot of time talking to clients (or service users), you will get great insights into the market and how different strategic actions would play out on the front line.

- Never allow yourself to think that, because you are at or near the top of the organisation, you are smarter or more knowledgeable than those further away. Your organisation has hired well, hasn't it? Use the talent across the whole company to get different points of view and see things through new lenses. It will do wonders for the morale, loyalty and professional development of your employees to demonstrate your confidence in them by getting as much input as possible from across the organisation.

- Build a strategy appropriate to your organisational culture. If there is weak control from the top, keep it short, provide guidelines and a framework. If, on the other hand, there is rigid control of lower layers, get the detail done and get it right.

So, in a large organisation, the logistics of managing a strategic cycle can be a real problem. We have seen that, in most organisations, the overarching strategy should come from the top and, at the very least, influence the strategic work done in divisions, regions, functions and subsidiaries. This means that the strategy cycle has to be carefully designed, executed with precision and checked for effectiveness throughout. We'll look in Chapter 8 at the way that your strategy should be reviewed.

As Robert Filek (PWC, FTI Consulting) said: "Strategy without process is little more than a wish list."

Do you need a strategy at all?

Lastly, maybe we should consider whether the very idea of a strategy is out of date. We all know that the pace of change is incredibly fast, and it's hard to keep up. Perhaps a 3-year strategy will be useless because every element of the plan will be obsolete by the time we get to the end of the three year period. With agile techniques borrowed from the world of IT development, perhaps we can just set some goals and implement in such an agile fashion that no one needs to write a strategy paper ever again. Agile is an iterative approach to project management and software development that helps teams deliver value to their customers faster and with fewer issues. Instead of betting everything on a 'big bang' launch, an agile team delivers work in small but consumable increments.

In my opinion, this is wrong because to come up with any agile implementation, you need exactly the same disciplines as I have been talking about to ensure that you make the best possible decisions and deployments of resources. Orit Gadiesh, the chair of Bain and Company, agrees: "With the level of uncertainty we see today, more people are asking, how can you develop a strategy in a world that keeps changing so fast? They are afraid that a set of rigid principles will hinder their ability to react quickly. I argue that it is precisely at such times that you need a strategy."

The top 10 reasons for poor strategy

Before we move on, here is my 'top of the pops chart' showing what are the most frequent and obvious mistakes made when strategies are created and presented. How many of these do you recognise from your own work or what you see in your organisation?

1. No executive summary.

2. No meaningful analysis of current situation.

3. Unclear, ambiguous, unmeasurable or even no goals proposed.

4. Unclear what the strategy is going to be.

5. Strategy proposes no change at all.

6. Far too much content.

7. No actions defined or too many actions defined.

8. Strategy is not aligned with purpose or vision.

9. No management system or communications plan.

10. Strategy is put into a drawer and never executed.

Perhaps a simpler way of summarising these errors comes from Vince Lombardi, an American football coach: "Hope is not a strategy."

Some strategy papers I have seen have suffered from several – if not most – of these ailments. I'll deal with all these errors during the course of this book, and I hope that by the end, you will feel there is some basic guidance that you can use to avoid the pitfalls.

The next case study is interesting because it's about an organisation that didn't have a formal, documented strategy at all and yet was very successful.

Case Study – BHWG, a Digital Marketing Agency

I found out the history of this start-up from one of the founders, Chris Barraclough. Having started his career in the 80s, Chris met his future business partners Simon Hall, Elly Woolston and Duncan Gray. They formed BHWG in 1991. It went on to become one of the most successful Direct Marketing (DM) agencies of the 90s, being bought by Omnicom in the latter part of the decade and rebranded Proximity London.

Chris tells me: "I was founder and chair of two companies. The first, BHWG, was started by 5 of us in 1991 as a direct marketing agency that was 'setting new standards'. The sector was pretty amateurish in those days and failing to attract big brands into the world of data-driven marketing. We wanted to professionalise it and put data into a brand's broader marketing objectives."

By the early 90s, more and more corporations were capturing data about their clients – especially retailers and companies dealing with consumers (airlines, mobile phone companies etc.); however, very few of them had realised the possibilities for personalised marketing that these databases offered. In almost every case, the data was being used for transactional purposes only – in other words, to take orders, receive payment, deliver goods, provide warranties and so on. Few had grasped that each database represented a potential goldmine. Nowadays, we all expect that organisations use this data (and indeed GDPR legislation recognises how much and how frequently it is used), and personalised, targeted marketing is well established.

Importantly for BHWG, even the DM agencies that were operating successfully had not fully grasped the opportunity that new databases were offering. The five founders of BHWG had been schooled on the British Airways Executive Club, which in the late 80s/early 90s was one of the first truly data-driven marketing projects in Europe.

That experience helped BHWG to become the first major agency to align data to targeting and creative work in a way the traditional DM agencies didn't – they were still focused on maximising direct response from huge volumes – nor did traditional advertising agencies, who were still fixated by the one-size-fits all 30-second TV ad.

At the same time, new technology (laser printing) was allowing for infinite copy variations, so it was possible to tailor messaging to an individual. What made BHWG different was that they could tell a client what that message should be and when it should be delivered. Digital does the same but at speed.

Chris recalls: "I think we produced the first attrition model for Barclaycard, which showed that cardholders who stopped using their cards to pay for petrol were very likely to leave Barclaycard. So we put in a trigger programme of messaging to prevent this. All commonplace today, not so then. And to make it attractive to big brands, we dovetailed it with their overall marketing objectives (even though many brands were keeping data in a silo as a 'test')."

What made them so successful was this alliance of data and creative. Today, Proximity (the agency BHWG became) claim this, as do most agencies, digital or not.

Chris was kind enough to do a Q&A for me.

Q. What was your strategy, and how was it set?

A. Our strategy was always to align data to creative. Our ambition was to be biggest and best. That was the direction we all wanted to go because we understood it, and we believed it was the future. I'm not sure that was ever written down as such... Our new business presentations were always based on three pillars: Strategy, Creative, Delivery.

Of course, once you get something like this right, all sorts of opportunities come your way, but then you have to ask whether or not they fit your strategy. For example, much of the focus of the direct industry in the 80s and 90s was on production – data processing, print, lettershop, fulfilment etc. We had many opportunities to grow fast by buying businesses like these, but we never did. They weren't strategic or creative.

These were the early days of the database. We'd been exposed to its potential through our work on the British Airways Executive Club. That introduced us to the power of segmentation, personalisation, ROI and brand.

We knew we could take that thinking – gain insights from the data, develop a comms plan, produce tailored creative, analyse results – into almost every big brand. It was riding the wave before most had cottoned on.

We were **a bottom-up agency,** whereas advertising agencies were top-down. Our campaigns were driven by what customer data was telling us. Advertising agency campaigns were led by what the brand wanted to say. That's a bit simplistic but, in essence, the truth.

Q. How was the strategy documented?

A. I'm not sure it was. However, we were a massive new business machine. In every pitch and credentials presentation, our strategy was reiterated and explained live to a client, the majority of whom bought it; our staff were in no doubt as to what we were trying to do.

Q. What were the goals? How did you measure progress?

A. The goal was to survive. And then to grow. We never sat down and said: "This is where we want to be in 5 years." We were growing so fast the whole business was a week to week thing. Very exciting but breathless.

I don't think we measured progress in any methodical way. We would keep an eye on things like agency rankings in the industry press, and awards won. Having the five founders still working on the business every day ensured continuity of strategy and culture.

We had strategy away days for the board to bring them up to speed and discuss what to do next. I can't help feeling, though, that these were probably lip service to the idea of involvement. They were also a chance to unwind for 24 hours, which in many ways was probably more valuable.

Q. What trade-offs were necessary?

A. In a small growing business, you live the strategy on a daily basis. And you cannot be too precious about it. You have to live, so our view was that if a client wanted to use us but perhaps did not fit the data / creative strategy, we would sometimes have to take them. PC World was an example of this at the time. A traditional retailer whose advertising wasn't really driven by the database.

Q. What were the difficult or contentious decisions?

A. Absorbing or buying other companies. This never really worked well as cultures were very different. For instance, the group (BBDO) wanted to consolidate their below the line ['below the line' is marketing jargon for direct marketing, as opposed to 'above the line', which is advertising] agencies into one. They did, but a Sales Promotion [SP] agency, for example, is not a database-driven organisation even if there are elements of SP in direct. I don't think these worked well for anyone.

Changing the name was a difficult decision for emotional reasons but the right thing to do. To build a worldwide group, there had to be a name that worked universally. Hence Proximity.

Q. How did it play out? What happened?

A. It worked beyond any of our wildest dreams. We were riding the crest of a wave as more and more businesses began investing in their databases for marketing purposes, as well as administrative ones.

In 1991 we started with five of us in Simon's parents' front room. I think the initial investment was £25k between us with a £75k loan from the bank. We sold the business to AMV BBDO four years later for many, many multiples of that figure. I stayed at Proximity until 2003.

At the peak, we employed 300+ staff, and major clients included The AA, Alliance & Leicester, Barclaycard, British

Red Cross, BT, Dove, Lloyds Bank, Pedigree Petfoods, Persil, Pepsi, PG Tips, RNLI, Royal Mail, Sainsbury's, Shell, Thomas Cook, TV Licensing, Volkswagen plus many others.

Q. What would you do differently with the benefit of hindsight, both in the content of the strategy and the way it was created etc.?

A. We should have written it down and formalised many more things. We had very little structure to anything, but events were happening too quickly. I note that by early 1995 we were already claiming 80 staff and 250 just three years later… expansion was rapid.

We never got the chance to stop and take stock. Even our board advisor used to tell us to slow down on the new business front and consolidate for a time. But there were too many good opportunities to do that. And having started with no money and no resources, we had an inbuilt fear of the work drying up or never appearing.

What I would advise anyone in that situation to do – with the benefit of hindsight – is to think more about what the exit plan is. We never worked out properly what we felt was the right way to hand over the business, and we would have benefited from having sat down to think it through.

[I find this ironic, given the number of times I have talked to enthusiastic MBA students who have built an entire exit strategy before they have thought of what business they even want to build. In every case, it involves making them very rich. I have yet to hear of one of them achieving this.]

Q. What happened to you after all this? Bring us up to date.

A. In the end, as often happens in growing businesses, I got too far removed from what I was good at and enjoyed doing. I loved doing the work and solving creative problems for clients. I didn't enjoy corporate occasions or group stuff; I believe the longer a job title, the less you do.

So in 2003, I left and set up a smaller business, very much with the same philosophy but more focused on comms for loyalty schemes and communications to existing customers.

Learnings:

It's a great example of a situational strategy. There was a gap in the market to be exploited, five talented people with insight gained from a very early adopter of the idea (BA) and the enthusiasm and nerve to set up a business to focus on that rapidly expanding gap. In this case – as it often is with fast-moving start-ups – the purpose and the strategy were essentially one and the same. There was no time to set goals and deep dive into the environment. They were swept up in what Geoffrey Moore calls the 'tornado'. This was an explosive market, and the one thing needed was to win new clients – as fast as possible and take market share. Chris talks of riding the wave.

The strategy was also very successful in that it focused the business on high-value activity. Chris described it as a 'thinking and creative business' which found much higher margins in ideas, insight and creativity than the traditional agency business of production, mechanics and media buying. The latter had become commodities, whereas the magical combination of experience and expertise in data analysis together with marketing creativity was – as the market showed – a winning formula and much harder to compete against.

The strategy was never written down. That's fine. It wasn't needed. Everyone knew exactly what to do and why. The purpose and the strategy were completely aligned and enacted in everyday business. With a relatively small number of employees, that's a recipe for success. Chris also pointed out that they not only knew what they wanted to do; they were equally clear on what they didn't want to do: the hallmark of a good strategy.

Interestingly, chatting to Chris revealed that when the agency was bought out by BBDO in 1995, they did need to start formalising their management system and then moved to a goal-oriented strategy, with specific targets from the parent company about contribution to their profit. This, in turn, led to more traditional strategic planning and operational plans.

Communicating the strategy was baked into business as usual. This is a fascinating example because of the fact that so many of the team (creative and sales) were involved in new client pitches. The presentations had to explain about this new agency and sell the agency as much as the product. So everyone both understood and could articulate the strategy. Chris described this as 'living it, not reading it'.

There seems to be a critical mass of employees (50-70 in Chris' opinion) where this approach simply can't be sustained. Above that number, the leaders are no longer in the day-to-day business in the way they could be at the start. They have to start managing as well as leading, and this is where the need for a formal planning process cuts in. It will be relatively simple to start with and – if the business does well enough – become very well established and documented.

The last point to consider before we move on is that while this book lays out some optimal approaches to writing a strategy, my experience is that no matter how hard one tries to do things 'right' when creating a strategy, in practice, it is a very different experience. If the supposedly ideal approach, as we will see later, is to perform a strategic analysis, formulate a strategic intent, and then define the strategic actions, it is seldom done as simply as that. Most organisations define some part of the strategy and then work around it – going backwards as they learn more, gain more insights and rework all the elements until finally, something emerges. Don't worry if this is how you work too – just keep the key elements in mind and avoid the pitfalls if you can.

A chair of one of the organisations I work with recently asked me: "How would we recognise the perfect strategy?" My view is that the perfect strategy is one that achieves consensus at the top of the organisation and then is whole-heartedly communicated, adopted by the staff and put into practice. Of course, there will be problems, faults and surprises. After all, you are trying to guess what the future looks like. Don't let that put you off trying to set the best possible course for your organisation.

Before we get into the details of strategy, we need to take a look at some of the foundations on which a strategy is built. I'll start with these in the next chapter.

Conclusions:

While it is a good idea to have a clear view of what we mean by 'strategy', there are many different types. The two kinds referred to in this book are situational and goal-based. Most strategies play out over a period longer than a year. In large organisations, setting strategy can be very complicated, accommodating divisions, regions and functions within an overall plan. Strategic planning takes time and effort; the return from having a strategy has to be greater than the cost of creating it. Many, if not most, companies make a lot of basic mistakes in writing strategies.

Tests before you start writing a strategy:

- Check that you know why you need a strategy.

- Ensure there are enough time and resources allocated to do a good job of writing it.

- Make sure you know how it will be created and used.

- Test that the person or group commissioning the work will also read and act on it.

- Test that the necessary collaboration between divisions, regions etc., is built into the process.

CHAPTER 2:

Strategy Foundations

"If you don't know where you are going,
you'll end up someplace else."

Yogi Berra (US baseball player and coach)

If you are going to build a good strategy, then, like building a house, it needs good foundations. These foundations allow you to find a strategy that is right for your organisation, and which is capable of being executed: the difference between a nicely written but theoretical paper and one that fits the way your company works and is capable of delivering what you need and expect.

In order to understand what I mean by foundations, we are going to have to dive into things like purpose, mission, vision, brand, governance, values... and others. What have these business buzzwords got to do with writing a strategy? Bear with me; I hope this chapter will make it clear.

In my experience, these are some of the most over-used and least understood bits of management jargon. If you search online for examples, you will quickly see that they are used interchangeably. This is a mistake, as they all have a part to play in business and specifically in building a strategy. If you get them right, they are a great basis for goal-setting and give a context for any strategies being created, and therefore are essential prerequisites for our thinking in this book.

Lastly, what you'll find is that – like every other 'rule' that I define – there are plenty of exceptions to how these terms are used. IKEA's vision statement, for example, is a statement of purpose combined with a vision. They refer to what I would call a mission statement as a 'business model'. That doesn't make them worse – or better – than conventionally labelled statements. We all know how successful IKEA has been. We should learn from them. *The labels are less important than the thinking behind them.* Clarity of thinking and clear, consistent communication will lead you to purpose, mission, vision and values whether you give them those labels or not.

Purpose

"It's only when companies are clear about their purpose, have clearly communicated it, and it is understood by the team that companies can achieve both unity of effort and distributed decision making."

Marc Koehler (Author of *Leading with Purpose*)

Purpose: *why* does your organisation exist? This is a very long-term view of your organisation. When, for example, a company is started, the purpose is very clear. It's to meet a market need better than anyone else, and usually, it's a very simple concept. When Amazon started in a garage in 1994, it just sold books.[3] Its purpose was clear and didn't need to be spelled out. Over time (at least 5 years, more likely 10-15), an organisation's purpose may change. A purpose gets to the heart of what makes your organisation distinctive (but not unique). An organisation's purpose may not always be written down. This is not necessarily a problem if there is a common understanding of it, and the behaviour of the organisation reflects that purpose. Unhappily, in some cases, the purpose has never been thought about, stated or communicated, because it is taken for granted.

This might happen because the founder of the business (or charity etc.) assumes that everyone else knows what the purpose is. But as the company has expanded into several layers of management, different geographies and perhaps new product lines, that original purpose has been lost or dissipated. Perhaps when that founder steps down, those taking up the reins may have to ask themselves what on earth the company that they lead is supposed to be doing. If it doesn't have a clear purpose, then any decision can seem like a good one.

A beginner's answer to the question about a company's purpose (and I have had this answer many times) is to say that it exists to make a profit. No. Definitely NO. Profits are just a way to make a business sustainable and ultimately to reward investors. If a business really thinks that its purpose is solely to make profit, it will rapidly go out of business because it will be directionless and purely mercenary, and no one wants to be part of that kind of company, whether as an employee, supplier, customer or business partner.

James C Collins (Author of *Good To Great*) sees purpose as having a much longer timescale and how important it is – but you will note that he doesn't distinguish between purpose and vision: "Purpose (which should last at least 100 years) should not be confused with specific goals or business strategies (which should change many times in 100 years). Whereas you might achieve a goal or complete a strategy, you cannot fulfil a purpose; it is like a guiding star on the horizon − forever pursued but never reached. Yet, although purpose itself does not change, it does inspire change. The very fact that purpose can never be fully realised means that an organisation can never stop stimulating change and progress."

What difference does it make to define the purpose of the organisation? Complex decisions are being made all the time... such as which investments to make from a long list of competing priorities.

- Which products to develop?

- Which markets to enter?

- Which acquisitions to make?

- Which mergers to consider?

- What skills are needed?

- What divestments are needed?

- Which elements of the brand are essential, and which are not?

All these questions are much harder to answer if you don't know − in detail − what the purpose of your organisation is. Many items on this list apply even if you are not working in a commercial organisation.

Consider, too, that a purpose will seldom state that a company is there to sell a particular product. If it does, one risks the 'Kodak' effect, where that well-known company disappeared when it could not reinvent itself for the digital era. Kodak became so dominant in photography that by 1976, 85% of all film cameras and 90% of all film sold in the US was Kodak.[4] The original vision statement of the founder, George Eastman, was 'to make photography as simple as using a pencil'.[5]

They had successfully followed a strategy similar to razor blade manufacturers: make the initial purchase low cost and profit from the follow-on purchases. However, the digital revolution turned this on its head, and losing sight of how digital cameras could continue to meet the original vision, they delayed the launch of their product – and by then, they had lost momentum and the market.

If they had truly followed their purpose, digital technology would have been an obvious direction to take as an early leader and visionary. John Kotter, in a 2012 Forbes article, attributes the failure to complacency founded on years of success. Indeed, sustained success is one of the enemies of real strategic thinking.[6]

Today's Kodak is a 'technology company focused on imaging'.

The reluctance to impinge on the success of their main product line, film, was not shared by any of their competitors. This is a big lesson for any company with an established set of customers. Don't count on their loyalty. They're customers, not (usually) your friends, and when a better offering comes along, it's in their interests to take it. Best to make it your offering, not a competitor's, that replaces your existing products.

If they had only remembered that they were supposed to make photography easier, they would have – perhaps – led the transition to digital.

One element of defining the company's purpose is to ask what is the enduring idea it has? IBM's enduring idea is 'world-changing progress'. I admire this answer very much. It does not tie IBM into what many people think it does – hardware – nor, indeed, any kind of technology. However, it is very likely that it will remain closely anchored to technology in order to deliver the progress that it sees as its enduring idea.

In actual fact, IBM's revenues from selling hardware have changed radically over the years. When I joined in 1981, over 99% of revenue came from hardware. When I left in 2019, this had fallen to just under 10%. Before the 1990s, the hardware frequently fulfilled the enduring idea, with products such as the Selectric typewriter and IBM PC making generations of workers more efficient. But the company never allowed itself to define 'world-changing progress' solely by hardware. There was considerable internal consternation when the PC division was sold to Lenovo. But it had served its purpose. It had, in its day, changed the world. Now world-changing progress is delivered through other products and services as well as hardware. It is a sign of IBM's clear understanding of its purpose that it can manage such a substantial change to its portfolio and still remain a formidable force in its industry.

Beware, however, of confusing organisational purpose with a slogan. Slogans – even clever ones – very seldom capture the purpose of an organisation in a handful of words. For years, IBM summarised its intent with the 'Smarter Planet' slogan. Really effective, much imitated and possibly one of its strongest ever campaigns. But that was never the same as IBM's purpose, which is longer-lasting, more subtle and nuanced.

A purpose should be defined in an exercise that results in a purpose statement – typically at least a couple of sentences and quite possibly a paragraph. In it, the company, charity etc., will state its enduring idea, who they serve, what makes them distinctive and some key thoughts about engagement with others. A purpose statement is not immutable but is probably the longest-lasting construct within an organisation. It should not be changed too often and certainly not lightly, and its effects should be continuous, consistent and persistent.

BMW define their purpose (which they call 'position', or 'what for') as: "*We take on business, environmental and societal challenges. We take responsibility for the mobility of tomorrow with a compelling offering and sustainable management.*"[7]

Compare that with their mission statement in the next section. I like the way they have done this. They have called their purpose the 'what for' and their mission the 'what'. It's fascinating that they see themselves first and foremost as problem-solvers – for business, the environment and society. It's only after that statement that they talk about mobility. This is a good purpose statement that will have a great chance of standing the test of time. You can also see how this can inform their decisions about strategy, hiring, leadership, communications, branding and so on. That's what a purpose statement is for.

Defining the organisational purpose is time-consuming, complicated and often contentious. Having said that, it can also be exciting and insightful. There are plenty of methodologies that can help this work, and there isn't room in this book to go into how it can be done. The bottom line is that it is an essential piece of work if you don't have a clear understanding of the purpose of your organisation.

As Boston Consulting Group says (*"Getting Uncomfortable On Purpose", 2019*): "Purpose should lead you in unusual directions. A purpose should prompt action in new directions rather than just summarising and preserving the status quo." This will only happen, though, if there is a deep and widely shared understanding of the purpose.

Lastly, a sense of purpose has a very different effect within an organisation – and that is to imbue the employees with a clear sense of *why* they work there and to provide strong motivation for those employees to contribute to the success of the organisation.

Case Study: Tesla

Let's take a closer look at Tesla. A fascinating company that was founded in 2003, and within the seventeen years since then, has become the most valuable car company on the planet. In July 2020, the stock price reached $498 per share and gave Tesla a capitalisation of $208bn, overtaking Toyota which was valued at $203bn. Astonishingly, in the first quarter of 2020, Tesla produced just 5% of the number of cars that Toyota did (103,000 versus 1.98 million).

What is so special about this company, and what can we tell about their strategy?

As we saw earlier, Tesla's purpose is: *"To accelerate the world's transition to sustainable energy."* The first thing to note is that this says nothing whatsoever about making cars. Did you know that Tesla also makes batteries to store mains electricity and that they make roof tiles that generate solar electricity as well?

They have three battery lines:

- Domestic and residential use (Powerwall).
- Powerpack for commercial companies.
- Megapack for utilities.

Elon Musk grabbed the headlines in 2017 when he bet the South Australian state government that Tesla could build and install the world's largest battery in less than 100 days from contract signature. The bet: if he didn't succeed, the battery would be free. The battery was up and running well before the deadline and has been a huge success.

The most obvious elements of a differentiated sales strategy from the car business are to sell direct, to set up a network of service centres, and to set up a charging infrastructure. These alone have up-ended the traditional car market, where cars are sold and serviced through dealer networks and the supply of fuel is of no interest to the car manufacturers.

Each of these is extraordinary for a mass-produced car. Selling direct is not easy with such an expensive product. Tesla actually closed showrooms and saw sales rocket.

In some ways, we can see Tesla as a carbon-free generation and storage company with a very big car manufacturing capability attached. If we look at their acquisitions, they are very much about battery technology. For example, in February 2019, Tesla announced that they would acquire Maxwell Technologies, a battery-tech company, for $218m. The other big acquisition from 2019 was Hibar, a Canadian company that specialises in manufacturing automation that can be used for battery cells.

The element of Tesla's strategy that has attracted the most attention is that of its battery production. In their 'battery day' presentation on the 22nd of September, 2020, we can see several elements of a strategy emerging. The material from this presentation is downloadable.[8]

First of all, there is a strategic intent (see Chapter 5): "To achieve the transition to sustainable energy, we must produce more affordable EVs [Electric Vehicles] and energy storage, while building factories faster and with far less investment."

There are two strategic goals stated, both to be achieved by 2025:

1. Terawatt-hour scale battery production.

    To get to 20 TWhr of battery manufacture (a TWhr is a measure of battery capacity. For example, a Kilowatt-hour would mean a battery provides a kilowatt of power for one hour) with the current factory capacity would mean investment of $2 trillion and hiring 2.8 million employees. Clearly, this is unaffordable, so the strategy must address how the manufacturing plants will change.

2. Halve the cost of battery production.

    Battery price is measured in dollars per Kilowatt Hour. An electric car might have a battery capacity of between 30 and 80 KWhr. Currently, (July 2021) batteries cost about $150 per KWhr. So an 80 KWhr battery would cost $12,000 to manufacture. Tesla's current cost per KWhr is a closely guarded secret but is estimated to be as low as $110 per KWhr. It is widely thought that a price of $100 per KWhr would provide purchase price parity with a conventional car. Getting to $55 would mean Tesla could price aggressively and still expand margins.

We have a strategic intent and two very specific goals. What are the strategic actions (see Chapter 6) to meet these goals?

Then there are 5 action areas given:

1. Cell design.
2. Cell factory.
3. Anode materials.
4. Cathode materials.
5. Cell vehicle integration.

Each of these contributes to meeting the stated goals. The presentation details the part each strategic action plays in delivering the following:

- 54% increase in range.

- 56% reduction in cost per KWhr.

- 69% reduction in manufacturing cost per KWhr.

We, therefore, have the key elements of a strategy in place. I am going to assume that the strategic analysis is sound; there are only a few charts in the presentation that show the analysis outputs. There is a clearly stated strategic intent and there are five strategic actions.

Is the strategy credible? The industry reaction has been very positive, despite disappointment over the lack of an announcement of a million-mile battery, which had been widely expected.

Given Tesla – and Elon Musk's – track record, it is quite possible that they can continue to rewrite the rules of the car market – oddly enough with a company purpose that says nothing about cars.

Learnings:

The strategy shows the importance of purpose in providing the basis for a distinctive plan. Tesla's purpose informs not just their strategy but also their acquisitions, their brand, and it attracts people who like the idea of working for a company that makes cars, batteries and solar tiles with the intent of reducing harmful emissions.

The strategy contains the elements that we would expect to see: strategic intent and strategic actions, with two well-defined goals.

The communication – like so much of Tesla's work – is brilliantly done. While Elon Musk may gain a lot of attention, the quality of the website is excellent, the language engaging and simple, and the graphics are the highest quality. Anyone can download the presentation that has been referred to here.

Most companies aren't like Tesla and won't ever be, but that doesn't mean that there are no lessons to learn for others.

Mission

"Without a mission statement, you may get to the top of the ladder and then realise it was leaning against the wrong building!"

Dave Ramsey (Author and broadcaster)

A mission is the manifestation of the purpose but may change more frequently. It can be expressed as specific long-term goals or may be less clear.

Because purpose and mission are so often confused, when we look at mission statements, it is obvious that some organisations conflate them with their purpose. Understanding the difference is an important step to setting the foundations on which the strategy is built (see Figure 2, *The House of Strategy*).

Purpose and mission are not dissimilar, nor are they the same thing. In simple terms, the purpose of an organisation is *why it exists*, while the mission statement states *what it does*. The reason for drawing this distinction is that a company can radically change what it does while still serving the same purpose.

To illustrate the difference between the two, let's look at an example.

A political party has a purpose. For the UK Labour party: "Its purpose is to organise and maintain in parliament and in the country a political Labour party" (The Labour party 2019 rulebook).[9] Note that this states nothing about being in power at either a national or local level. That in itself tells us something about the nature of a purpose statement and how it contrasts with an organisation's mission.

There isn't a mission statement that I can find for the Labour party, but it would be a reasonable assumption that its mission would be to regroup after the 2019 UK election result and achieve a majority in parliament, or, failing that, to win enough seats to form a minority government. Thus purpose and mission are tangibly different.

Here are some examples of mission statements:

- Amazon: "When Amazon.com launched in 1995, it was with the mission "to be Earth's most customer-centric company – where customers can find and discover anything they might want to buy online – and endeavour to offer its customers the lowest possible prices." This goal still applies today, but Amazon's customer base is now worldwide and has grown to include millions of consumers, sellers, content creators, developers and businesses. Each of those groups has different needs, and we always work to meet those needs by innovating new solutions to make things easier, faster, better and more cost-effective."[10]

- BMW: "We offer inspiring premium products and premium services for individual mobility. Today and for future generations. We ensure high profitability so we can independently shape the future of mobility."[11]

Take a close look at the Amazon mission statement. It's awkward, isn't it? That's because, in addition to the familiar online shopping Amazon, they have a second – enormous – business called AWS that provides cloud services for developers and companies. The clumsy mission statement is an attempt to rationalise such different businesses. If Amazon is going to end up as more than a holding company for a bunch of disparate businesses, then it needs to think what – at core – its mission actually is.

Contrast that with BMW's concise and precise wording. The more I have looked at it, the more I have come to admire it. Probably, you think of BMW as a producer of cars for an upper-middle-class demographic. A few of you may realise they also produce motorcycles. But that's not how they define their mission. They clearly position themselves by the use of the word 'premium', but they don't say what their mobility products or services have to be. But it is clear that they are about allowing/helping *individuals* to be mobile. They also keep an eye on the future by talking about future generations, which brings in sustainability, as well as innovative product development. Lastly, they ensure that profitability is not forgotten so they can sustain their business for the future. Combined with the purpose statement we just looked at, I am confident that this mission statement will be one that lasts longer than most. It is – in my opinion – much more effective than Amazon's mission statement.

Note also that neither of these mission statements ties these companies into specific products or channels. They have the freedom to explore many options before they need to revisit these statements.

The best mission statements are much more likely to be expressed as a single sentence or even a short slogan. We have contrasting examples from Amazon and BMW, but let's take a look at some more:

IKEA have a 'business idea', which reads: *"To offer a wide range of well-designed, functional home furnishing products at prices so low, that as many people as possible will be able to afford them."[12]*

If you are thinking about how to write your own mission statement, a hint that I usually suggest is to take your organisation name out of the statement and see if you and others can tell who the statement refers to. These examples may or may not pass that test.

Vision

"A vision without a strategy remains an illusion."

Lee Bolman (Author of books on leadership)

A vision, in our context, is a corporate statement providing organisational direction toward a desired state for that entity and its customers/service users.

- Oxfam's vision: *"Nine billion people will live equitably and free from the injustice of poverty, on a planet that has the natural resources to sustain them."[13]*

- BMW's vision: *"To create innovations."[14]*

- IKEA's vision: *"We have a passion for life at home. Our culture is built upon enthusiasm, togetherness and a "get-it-done" attitude. We're optimists, constantly looking for new and better ways to do things, from how to design a rocking chair that fits into a flat-pack to creating LED light bulbs that are affordable to everyone. Our vision is to create a better everyday life for the many people – for customers, but also for our co-workers and the people who work at our suppliers."[15]*

Is the organisation's vision the same as its overarching goal? Or perhaps it can be its strategic intent. The answer is no – to both. It can't substitute for a goal as it's not nearly specific enough, on purpose. Goals need to be SMART. Goals also may need to change, but the vision should sustain the organisation through changes of strategy, leadership and execution. It can't be the strategic intent either because that is about defining what the strategy involves: what you are going to do about either the situation or about meeting the goals.

The very essence of a vision statement is that it should be unachievable but inspire a sense of purpose for those in the organisation (and customers, suppliers and other stakeholders too) that motivates. As we will see in the chapter on communicating the strategy, instilling a sense of purpose is an important part of getting the strategy executed. Steve Jobs knew the power of a good vision: "If you are working on something exciting that you really care about, you don't have to be pushed. The vision pulls you."

The vision statement should, of course, be informed by the purpose of the organisation. The better understood the latter is, the easier it will be to create the right vision.

I think of vision statements as being like the carrot on a stick for the donkey (not a very flattering analogy, of course!). No matter how hard the organisation strives, it will never quite get there.

When writing the strategy, the vision is perhaps the easiest thing to link to, as the strategy should be very clear about how the strategic intent and strategic actions (discussed in Chapters 5 and 6) strain to achieve the vision.

Values

> "Your habits become your values; your values
> become your destiny."

Mario Tomasello (Data Scientist)

Values relate to the culture of the organisation. It's the essence of the people who work there. How do they behave when no one's looking? Or what happens when there is a clash between a client's genuine needs and the rules or processes that govern what you do?

We know that it's not as easy as 'the customer is always right' because when that customer is making unreasonable demands, it's not OK just to say yes. However, suppose that client is having a crisis – business or personal – then it may not be good enough to rely on business as usual. That's where values kick in to inform us what the best answer is, rather than the 'right' answer. Employees living up to the organisational values can provide the very best differentiation between one company and another. IBM, for example, believes that its sustainable competitive advantage is its values.

Some examples:

Amazon's values are expressed as leadership principles.[16] "We use our leadership principles every day, whether we're discussing ideas for new projects or deciding on the best approach to solving a problem. It is just one of the things that makes Amazon peculiar."

Leaders:

Customer obsession; Ownership; Invent and simplify; Are right, A lot; Hire and develop the best; Insist on the highest standards; Think big; bias for action; Frugality; Vocally self-critical; Earn trust of others; Dive deep; Have backbone; Disagree and commit; Deliver results.

When I look at these, I see far too many to use as values. They are potentially mutually contradictory (how does 'Insist on the highest standards' sit with 'frugality', for example?); they aren't going to be remembered. Each has explanatory text. I have just reproduced the headlines.

The Nolan Principles[8] for public office holders in the UK are:

Selflessness, integrity, objectivity, accountability, openness, honesty and leadership.

My previous employer, IBM's values:[17]

- Dedication to every client's success.

- Innovation that matters – for our company and the world.

- Trust and personal responsibility in all relationships.

I sit on the board at Southern Health NHS Foundation Trust, whose values are:[18]

- Patients and people first.

- Respect.

- Trust.

In each case, there are more detailed explanations that I haven't reproduced about what these mean in practice. However, none of the explanations could be interpreted as required behaviours for employees. It's not about how to adhere to the employee conditions of employment; it's about how to *break the rules*. Essentially, it's the moral choices to make as opposed to staying within the legal boundaries set. If an employee stays within the legal requirements, they can't be sacked, but they will be – at best – unimaginative and probably uncommitted.

I favour a shorter number of values, simply expressed, because these are meant to cover the parts where job definitions and processes don't help or are counter-productive. Detailed instructions are unhelpful because they end up trying to be prescriptive. The whole point of values is that they are there to guide when the normal prescriptions don't help.

Let's look at Unilever, whom I regard as a very principled company, thanks to the farsightedness of their former chief executive, Paul Polman.

Their values:[19]

1. Always working with integrity

   Conducting our operations with integrity and with respect for the many people, organisations and environments our business touches has always been at the heart of our corporate responsibility.

2. Positive impact

   We aim to make a positive impact in many ways: through our brands, our commercial operations and relationships, through voluntary contributions, and through the various other ways in which we engage with society.

3. Continuous commitment

   We're also committed to continuously improving the way we manage our environmental impacts and are working towards our longer-term goal of developing a sustainable business.

4. Setting out our aspirations

   Our Corporate Purpose sets out our aspirations in running our business. It's underpinned by our Code of Business Principles which describes the operational standards that everyone at Unilever follows, wherever they are in the world. The Code also supports our approach to governance and corporate responsibility.

5. Working with others

   We want to work with suppliers who have values similar to our own and work to the same standards we do. Our Supplier Code, aligned to our own Code of Business Principles, comprises eleven principles covering business integrity and responsibilities relating to employees, consumers and the environment.

Now we can contrast their values with those of their principal competitor, P&G.[20]

1. Integrity

   We always try to do the right thing.

   We are honest and straightforward with each other.

   We operate within the letter and spirit of the law.

   We uphold the values and principles of P&G in every action and decision.

   We are data-based and intellectually honest in advocating proposals, including recognising risks.

2. Leadership

   We are all leaders in our area of responsibility, with a deep commitment to delivering leadership results.

   We have a clear vision of where we are going.

We focus our resources to achieve leadership objectives and strategies.

We develop the capability to deliver our strategies and eliminate organisational barriers.

3. Ownership

   We accept personal accountability to meet our business needs, improve our systems and help others improve their effectiveness.

   We all act like owners, treating the company's assets as our own and behaving with the company's long-term success in mind.

4. Passion for Winning

   We are determined to be the best at doing what matters most.

   We have a healthy dissatisfaction with the status quo.

   We have a compelling desire to improve and to win in the marketplace.

5. Trust

   We respect our P&G colleagues, customers and consumers, and treat them as we want to be treated.

   We have confidence in each other's capabilities and intentions.

   We believe that people work best when there is a foundation of trust.

I've reproduced both companies' value statements in full because it provides a fascinating contrast. Unilever chooses some interesting words: 'society', 'voluntary' and 'sustainable' are all clear pointers. If you didn't know whose values they were, you might be able to guess.

Notice that P&G don't mention the environment or society at all. If we took the 'P&G' out of the statements, I think you might find it difficult to know which organisation had written them. In my opinion, P&G missed an opportunity to make themselves more distinctive.

You'll also find companies talking about principles. This sometimes translates to values; on other occasions, it means the employee behaviour guidelines or requirements. For example, Unilever's principles come under 14 headings, each with explanatory text.[21]

There is a relationship between values and culture, of course. Culture is discussed in the next section, but we can think of values – as written down for an organisation – as the cultural aspiration and culture as the reality.

Values, in conclusion, need to be short, hard to define, difficult to prescribe and – like purpose and mission – distinctive. They give permission to depart from the normal process when it is better for the organisation.

Culture

"I came to see, in my time at IBM, that culture isn't just one aspect of the game – it is the game. In the end, an organisation is nothing more than the collective capacity of its people to create value."

Lou Gerstner (former chair and CEO of IBM)

Culture is, in many ways, the hardest of all these elements to pin down and measure. But it's probably going to be the most important factor in the execution of your strategy. If creating a strategy is almost entirely a rational process, getting to grips with and changing culture is the opposite.

The reason that culture is so hard to get to grips with is that it's not written down anywhere. If something is written down, it's almost certainly not part of the culture. Think of it as the subconscious behaviour that dictates responses; Daniel Kahneman's System 1 behaviour (See *Thinking, Fast and Slow*). It's fast, automatic, happens unconsciously and requires minimal effort. System 2, in contrast, is slower, requires effort, and happens consciously and deliberately. While these systems describe individual behaviours, they can be applied to how strategy relates to culture. Strategy is created through a System 2 process. It's deliberate, thoughtful and consciously focuses on data, evidence and reasoned thinking.

Culture is how the organisation will respond to your strategy. Does what you are asking people to do fit with the company culture? If it does, then the strategy will appear 'natural' to people. It will fit their preconceptions of how they and their colleagues work. On the other hand, if you need them to behave in a totally different way, then you will create some discomfort, unease, and potentially resistance to your plans. This resistance may be deliberate and overt ('we just don't work that way'), or it may be unintentional or covert ('we're trying to do what you asked, but it simply doesn't work').

How do cultures emerge? The starting point may be that a successful organisation encourages behaviours that appear to reinforce success. This may be like a superstition: a coincidental match between success and a pattern of behaviour is sustained because of the correlation, despite the fact that this correlation may not, in fact, be the cause of the success. Initially, at least, the behaviours bring success and promotions for those who follow this template. So, there are visible rewards for both the company and for individuals who fall into this pattern. This may not be a bad thing at all. It may be that the culture reinforces professional behaviour, integrity and hard work.

But there is a risk that the culture becomes fixed and fossilised and no longer serves the organisation as it once did. For example, if the culture is one of formality (wearing formal business attire, stuffy meetings, bureaucracy), then it may put off talented people from joining who see it as old-fashioned and likely to discriminate. It may find that its potential customers want a faster-moving, more casual and friendly company to deal with.

How deeply embedded is a culture? I see it as being largely dictated by two dimensions: first, the longevity/history of the organisation and the number of employees. Of course, this is an oversimplification, but it points to two of the major components. If you are part of a company or charity that has existed for – say – two hundred years, there will be elements of culture that are rooted – deeply, in some cases – in the history of the organisation. Having survived that long, it has clearly been doing some things right. There will probably be a culture of client service, employee loyalty, consistency and so on. I can't think of many very large organisations that are this old, with the possible exception of the armed services.

The second element is that of size (using employee numbers as the measure). The reason for this is that if a very large organisation has a strong culture, then the amount of effort needed to change that becomes enormous and certainly daunting. Returning to our example of IBM, a company that is about 110 years old and has something like 400,000 employees around the world. Lou Gerstner commented: "...changing the attitude and behaviour of hundreds of thousands of people is very, very hard to accomplish. Business schools don't teach you how to do it... You can't mandate it; you can't engineer it."

One other thing about culture is that it's very difficult to measure – if not impossible. You can create all kinds of proxies that can be measured, but that doesn't get to the heart of the issue.

If the culture has become out of tune with the times, the needs of clients and of employees, then changes need to be made. Of all the changes to corporations, culture change is the slowest and hardest, in my experience. It's not like changing a process or the employee handbook. If the culture change can be an evolution that has some consistency with previous behaviours, it will be easier. It's like a river flow – if you create a new passage for the water, it will flow into it naturally. If you just build a dam, eventually the water will go over the top or around it. It's even harder to get the water to flow uphill – that requires a big pump and a lot of energy.

To make changes, the whole executive team must be fully committed to the new attributes of the culture that you want to engender. One person who sticks to the old agenda can undermine the entire effort. The execs must change their own behaviours and be seen to do so. They need to encourage and reward those who exhibit the right approach and coach those who do not.

In a large organisation, senior appointments give a clear message to the organisation of who is doing well, and those promoted into senior positions must be seen as champions of the new cultural approach. It's also very noticeable that the leadership style at the top sets the style for the rest of the organisation. If the CEO behaves in a brusque, intolerant and overriding fashion, then don't be surprised if that management approach cascades down the company. On the other hand, if the CEO exemplifies the cultural values that you want adopted, then other leaders will also want to be seen to act in that way. Personal example is a very strong prerequisite for culture change. As a small example, if there is a problem of needing to be visible in the office, leading to everyone staying late in the office, but not doing valuable work, then the sight of the CEO leaving at 18:00 sends a powerful message that the leader won't be there to check who is staying late.

In such a company, or one with regular changes of leadership, the workforce might feel that they can simply sit tight and ride out the changes introduced by a new CEO. After all, CEOs don't usually last more than three or four years, and the long-lasting employees may have seen several over the years. If they know that they can ignore the changes and eventually the CEO will move on – or shift priorities – then there is little chance that the culture will change. It takes huge amounts of determination, persistence and personal commitment to make cultural change stick.

One last comment on culture: in my view, the healthiest organisations find a way to accommodate 'irritants' who are not, at first sight, a good fit with the culture. These are the mavericks who come up with wild ideas, constantly chafe within the constraints of the management system, but who push for change, call out the mistakes that others don't and who enable different approaches to be taken. These 'wild ducks' are a precious asset, and an organisation that values them and knows how to get the best from them will generally benefit hugely.

Brand

> "Your brand is what other people say about you
> when you're not in the room."
>
> **Jeff Bezos (CEO of Amazon)**

In my experience, there are few terms used more frequently in business – and outside it – than the word 'brand'. I very seldom find that it's used thoughtfully and with insight because branding is a complex and difficult thing to do. I was once lectured at length during a dinner party by someone who told me that a well-known charity should 'monetise its brand' in ways that were utterly inappropriate to that charity.

Like so many other topics in this book, there is a wealth of literature on the subject, and I don't intend to go into great detail, as it has been much better covered elsewhere. However, brand is an important part of the context for, and thinking about, strategy, so I need at least to cover the basics.

There appear to be as many definitions of brand as there are commenters. One of the first I came across was 'a product with a personality', which is fine, up to a point. In its simplest form, a brand is literally a mark used to show that an animal belongs to a particular farm (or ranch), often burned into an animal's hide. But it's come to mean much more than that.

There is something, usually physical (a logo, a sound – like Intel's infuriating and brilliant five note jingle) that elicits both a rational and an emotional response. We may not be aware of the emotional response, and we may not be aware of how it affects purchasing and giving decisions, but it is highly influential. Organisations spend huge amounts of money to define, protect and update their logos. If I wanted to reproduce a company logo here, I would need to get permission from that company to do so. I can type IBM, but they would need to agree before I could print their famous eight bar logo.

There is also a difference between a product brand (like Dove soap) and the brand of an organisation. Exploring the Dove example a little, it's a very carefully curated consumer product that has made a great deal of effort to make an emotional connection to its target audience: "For over a decade, we've been working to make beauty a source of confidence, not anxiety…" and if you take a look at the website, you have to scroll down through several impressive initiatives to find the first mention of a specific product.

An organisation's brand is more complex. Dove is owned by Unilever (although many of its customers may not know or care about this). Unilever's branding is totally separate – but there needs to be a match between the products it owns and its own brand. I've already discussed Unilever's values, which inform the actions it takes to manage its brand.

We know that a brand is potentially hugely valuable. Forbes values the Apple brand at over \$205bn and Google at \$168bn. Even number 100 in their list, Kellogg's, is valued at \$8bn.[22] It doesn't really matter how the valuation is calculated – the point is that these are incredibly powerful, as they have global recognition, strong emotional response and carry a very clear promise in the mind of the consumer.

One word of warning. There are a lot of marketing consultancies that specialise in brand strategy. The best of these are excellent at getting to the root of the organisation, understanding its purpose, culture, history and strategy and then attuning the branding to those underpinnings. Others, however, devote all their energies to a redesign of the logo, coming up with a neat slogan, obsessing about fonts and colours used, and so on. I'm not saying that these are unimportant, but they come at the very end of the branding process and should naturally follow on from the decisions taken earlier in the thinking. The most important thing in branding is conscious consistency, by which I mean you have thought through exactly what your brand is about and how, when and why its communications (in the broadest sense) are always aligned with the character of the organisation.

When you think about your brand, apply these tests to any communications, including face-to-face meetings:

- Does it *look* like your organisation?
- Does it *sound* like your organisation?
- Does it *think* like your organisation?
- Does it *perform* like your organisation?

How is your organisation *experienced*?

The point for us to consider is that any strategy needs to take into account the brand of the organisation it is for. Let's look at that in a bit more detail.

First of all, don't have a strategy that will damage the brand.

Let's look at the famous example of Coca Cola and the battle they had with Pepsi, leading to the disastrous launch of New Coke in 1987. Coca Cola had a long-running difficulty: in blind tastings, Pepsi consistently used to win. Consumers preferred the taste of Pepsi when they didn't know what they were drinking. Coca Cola's logic was that if they launched a product that blind-tasted better than Pepsi, in combination with one of the best-known logos and most capable marketing machines in the world, they would grab large chunks of market share. Unfortunately, New Coke bombed. There were public protests, bottle emptying in the streets, boycotts and hostile press coverage. Just 77 days later, Classic Coca Cola, with the original formula, was introduced, and the new formula was allowed to die quietly.

The lesson here is that Coca Cola is known for its visual brand, of course, but another element of its brand is its taste, and as Coca Cola found out, the emotional attachment to the brand was phenomenal. The new version just didn't taste like Coca Cola.

As an afterthought, Coca Cola's sales in North America recovered strongly when Classic was introduced, and the CMO, Sergio Zyman, decided that the whole exercise had been a resounding success: "... because it rekindled the relationship between the American public and Classic Coke." Interestingly for us, he continues by saying that: "the only reason it wasn't a disaster is that we were willing to learn from the experience and to change our minds."

So, Coca Cola's story tells us not to build a strategy that conflicts with the brand your organisation will have spent so much time, effort and probably money building.

More positively, if you can create a strategy that plays off the strength of the brand, then it is more likely to resonate, not just with consumers/customers, but also with employees, business partners, suppliers and the communities in which you are based. Don't think that the concept of having a brand is just for big organisations. As soon as you deliver a service, product, or work of any kind, you also deliver the impression of how you do it. Are your products reliable, high quality, delivered on time? Is your organisation honest, kind, generous, adaptable, etc.? The more that there is consistency of service/product and organisational behaviour, the sooner your brand will build – for good or ill. We can all think of examples of being willing to spend more on something because we associate positive ideas about the product. Supermarkets' own brands would be the only things sold on their shelves if we didn't value brands. Similarly, I am sure you can think of local tradespeople who you have a bad experience with, and wouldn't use again.

If you understand your brand: what's good about it; what's less good; what you are working to change, and what you need to maintain; then you can incorporate that thinking into your strategy and ensure that the brand supports the strategy and vice versa.

Let's look at a company that has aligned its strategy with its brand – Harley-Davidson. It was founded in 1903 and has products that elicit strong emotions. Some motorcyclists are completely passionate about their Harley-Davidson bikes, while others would never want to ride one.

HD's 2020 strategy statement read:

"We're on a quest to build the next generation of Harley-Davidson riders globally, with efforts focused on deepening rider engagement and commitment whether they're new to riding or seasoned road warriors. We're inspiring riders, expanding globally and investing to achieve profitable growth – all while playing our part in sustaining our planet."

What's interesting about this statement are the phrases 'deepening rider engagement and commitment', 'whether new to riding or seasoned road warriors' and 'inspiring riders'. It's all about the emotional reaction; we don't get performance figures, racing success, speed or horsepower from HD.

Their first objective – neatly defined with a date and a numerical objective, is to expand total Harley-Davidson riders to 4 million in the US by 2027. Again, note the words used in the detail of the objective (my emphasis):

"Building committed riders is critical to our future and we're focused on attracting new riders and keeping all riders riding, **inspiring passion and commitment** along the rider journey."[23]

A strategy that is aligned well with the brand will seem natural, and it will be hard to see the joins between the company strategy and the brand strategy; it's when they are not working together in harmony that the 'feel' will be all wrong.

Governance

"Governance is the framework of authority and
accountability that defines and controls the outputs,
outcomes and benefits from projects, programmes
and portfolios."

Association For Project Management

Governance has become an overused term. It has a very specific meaning, and I am going to use the definition offered by the Chartered Institute of Governance.[24]

"Corporate governance is the system of rules, practices and processes by which a company is directed and controlled."

Don't confuse governance with management – the terms are often (mis-)used interchangeably. Management is about the day-to-day running of the organisation, from top to bottom.

Stakeholders, such as shareholders, investors, suppliers, staff etc., need confidence that the organisation is run according to the best principles and practices, including transparency, appropriate business controls and reporting. Good governance ensures, for example, that conflicts of interest are avoided where possible and openly declared if unavoidable. Governance also ensures that the organisation's leadership develops plans that are compatible with the ethical, legal and regulatory standards expected of that industry.

The processes for setting and pursuing the company's objectives, which are part of good governance, are right at the heart of defining a strategy. So how does governance manifest itself when thinking about strategy? The most obvious example is the board. In the UK, most boards are unitary boards: executive and non-executive directors sit on the same board and are jointly accountable for the sustainability and performance of the organisation. The US often has separate boards of executive and non-executives. As with so many things in organisations, there is no right and wrong here, but you need to understand the way in which the oversight of the organisation affects not so much what you write but how approval is given to the strategy. I would expect any significant strategy work affecting the whole organisation to be seen and approved by the board(s). Non-executive directors should be bringing constructive but critical thinking to the assessment of the strategy, as well as expertise based on their skills and experience.

The board may have been involved in the circumstances from which the strategy is built. Perhaps it set some strategic goals that the strategy must address; perhaps its view of the industry or environment has led to a desire for a situational strategy to be developed. Either way, I see the board as a fundamental part of strategy design, development, approval and communication. If you feel that the board is there to rubber-stamp your work, then something is wrong.

This is why, in Figure 2, *The House Of Strategy*, governance is shown as affecting the house of strategy from top to bottom. Effective governance is going to be a great help to you; ineffective oversight will be a hindrance: too much interference, operational interventions from non-executives, disconnects between execs and non-execs will all make the job harder.

Putting it all together: 'The House of Strategy'

So how do these elements all fit together, and how do they relate to the strategy? I imagine them fitting together as one would build a house. A good house needs solid foundations, and the purpose represents the underpinnings of the strategy. Without a good understanding of purpose, it is unlikely that you will ever build a solid strategy. It isn't necessary to have a carefully crafted purpose statement, especially if you are a small charity or business. However, it IS essential to know your purpose and be very clear in your own mind about what it tells you. Formally writing it down is a valuable exercise and can lead to fascinating insights into the organisation. If you are big enough to have several layers of management, I strongly recommend that you take the time and trouble to create and share a formal purpose statement.

If you have understood the purpose, then it will act as a touchstone for the key directions that you set in the strategy, which need to take you somewhere that is consistent with your purpose.

Purpose should be the unifying factor when linking strategies between different divisions, functions and areas. Unless they are totally separate (like GE divisions), then they need to share a purpose.

The purpose statement then leads clearly to the mission statement and the vision statement. The vision statement shows what the world will be like if you fulfil your purpose. The mission statement starts to make the purpose more concrete: 'If this is our purpose, then we have to achieve...'

...and the goals then follow naturally to enable you to turn the mission into specific goals with dates and measurements.

Now we have the foundations of the strategy. The strategy – which we'll cover in later chapters – in turn, leads to operational goals and an operating plan. The period for operational goals and the operating plan will depend on your organisation, but let's generalise and say that the operating plan covers the current year.

The roof is provided by the brand. In times of 'bad weather', it can provide great shelter, but it's essential to maintain your roof/brand so that it's strong and reliable. Whatever you do, don't let your strategy damage your brand or the rain will pour in.

Surrounding the 'house of strategy' are the organisational culture and values. Every part of the house should be consistent with the values – if not, a tension will be created that could prove fatal to what you are trying to do.

Governance is 'insurance for buildings and contents' that makes sure that the organisation is run in accordance with good practice, sets out what happens in specific circumstances and ensures there is no disconnect between the stakeholders and management.

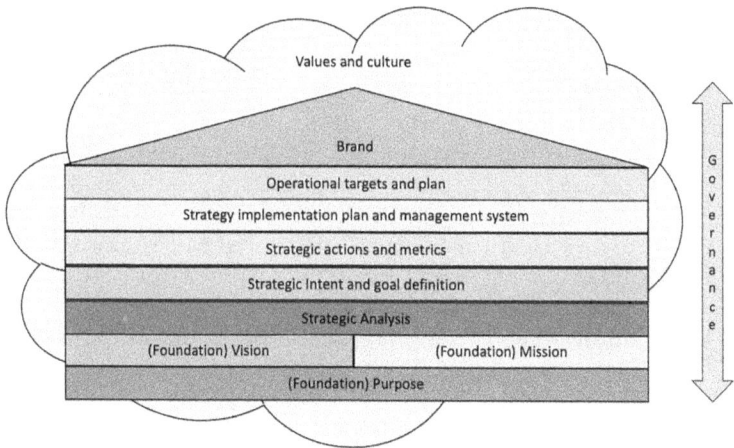

Figure 2. The House of Strategy.

Working from the bottom up, each 'floor' in the house is a prerequisite to the layer above it. Creating strong foundations (purpose, vision, mission) means that the structure built on those foundations will be sturdy and long-lasting.

This picture can represent the whole organisation, or a part of it. If it is a subset of the organisation, good management practices will ensure that each element accurately reflects the intentions and needs of the broader structure.

Conclusions:

Like any plan, a strategy needs firm foundations. If you think of a strategy as a way of achieving a specific end, then you need to be confident that you have selected the right goal. A deep understanding of the purpose of your organisation will give confidence in this. Your strategy needs to fit the purpose, vision and mission that have been established and be consistent with the culture, values and brand of your company. The more you stray from these foundations, the less likely you are to succeed in executing your strategy.

Tests for writing a strategy:

1. Has your organisation defined its purpose, vision and mission?

2. Are they clearly articulated and shared widely amongst the employees?

3. Can all levels of employees describe them and how their work contributes to them?

4. Can you see what limitations your purpose imposes on your strategy?

5. Has your organisation stated its values, and do you understand how these relate to the culture?

6. How does the organisational culture affect the way that the strategy can or should be implemented?

CHAPTER 3:

Goals

"Sound strategy starts with having the right goal."

Michael Porter (Academic, business author, advisor and speaker)

Why are goals important?

A strategy needs to be evaluated on how well it is working. That implies you are measuring what improvements have been made over the period of execution of the strategy. However, without goals, the organisation does not know how to allocate its resources to prioritising progress in specific areas. It does not have a mechanism to declare 'success'. Working out what the right goals are is discussed in more detail later. Let's have a look at how strategic goals might be set.

While we are discussing goals, you will often hear references also to targets, objectives and possibly OKRs (Objectives and Key Results). For the purposes of this book, I will use them as follows:

Goal: overarching achievement for a strategy

Target: a short(er) term and more tactical outcome

Objective: depends on context, can be either

OKRs: measurement system to unify a company or team on the same intended outcome

SMART goals (or targets)

Useful goals tend to have specific characteristics. They are:

1. Specific: provide a clear description of what needs to be achieved

2. Measurable: define how you will measure the achievement of the goal

3. Attainable: set an ambitious goal at a level that motivates but not so high that your organisation turns off

4. Realistic*: set a goal that your organisation is **ready** and **willing** to achieve

5. Time-bound: set an unambiguous date for achieving the goal

* Sometimes the 'R' is defined as 'Relevant', meaning that the goal should be consistent with the organisation's broader objectives.

...or SMART... or SMARRT.

What happens if your goal(s) are extremely hard to measure accurately? A classic example is for improving the image of a company (or charity etc.). How are you going to measure this? Some companies with hundreds of thousands, or millions, of customers can get solid metrics for (e.g.) Net Promoter Score, which is one part of the image. It's possible to get analytics for social media sentiment, which is another element. You can look at mainstream press (or industry media) for what they say; you can analyse what the most influential commentators ('influencers') say about you. There is no one measurement that gives the answer; you will need to decide which are best for you.

The message here is that you need to find a way to measure progress. Sometimes this will be several measures on a scorecard; sometimes, you will find a single metric that your stakeholders will accept. Some measures will feel a long way from where you want to be (a distant proxy). Be innovative in the way you measure such complex and challenging goals – but don't settle for vague generalities. Get objective, replicable and precise numbers that at least allow you to see a trend.

There's always a temptation to set fluffy or ambiguous goals so that one can argue later that the goals have been met, but that's an approach that dooms either the organisation or you to failure. It should be you, of course, but if your leader(s) let you get away with goals that are poorly defined, they should share the blame. The strategy review process allows for the goals to change, rightly so. Be precise, write the best strategy you can to meet those goals and then work to understand whether the strategy or the execution needs to be improved.

Sometimes the goals will be extremely challenging. This is often a good thing because it will force you to write a strategy that rethinks what the organisation is doing. A business as usual (BAU) strategy is going to produce – let's face it – BAU results. So, having goals that cannot be achieved by BAU behaviour is an opportunity to take a new, bold or radical approach to meeting the targets. This is the exciting part of strategising.

Setting goals

First, you may be the person setting them for the whole organisation. This may be because you are the CEO or owner of the business. Those would be good reasons to be setting the goals. You – together with whatever stakeholders you have – will decide what you want the organisation to achieve.

If, on the other hand, you have been given the task of writing the strategy for the organisation by your boss and part of that task is to set, or recommend, the goals – STOP. You're not the right person to be deciding on the goals. You will fail, or attract criticism, either sooner (because the goals don't have executive buy-in) or later (because events show that they were not bold enough or too bold). This is a no-win. Start the strategy when the goals are clear and have complete buy-in from the top, and not before.

Secondly, you may be setting the goals for a division, function or geography. An example of each would be the retail arm of a bank, the HR function of a large NHS Trust or the European wing of a large multinational. Buy-in is critical. You may be handed the targets or may have the leeway to decide your own. Buy-in comes with the targets that are given to you – in other words, you know your management agree the targets. If you create your own, take time and trouble to understand what they should be:

- Will they satisfy your stakeholders?
- Are they consistent with the wider organisation's goals and strategy?
- Are they clear and unambiguous?
- Are they bold enough?
- And then, are they SMART?

Long-term v short-term goals

Are we talking about long-term goals? In most cases, yes. Strategic goals tend to be objectives that are to be achieved in the medium term: say 2-5 years out. 'Ah', I hear you say, 'Five years out is subject to so many variables that there's no point in even setting goals for that period'. There's some truth in that, and whether there is any point will depend on the nature of your organisation. If you are a small start-up, then setting 12 month goals might be as far as you can or should go. However, you may equally decide that within five years, you want to have built the business to a point where you can sell some or all of your stake. That's a pretty common long-term goal, and you will definitely need to have an idea of what condition the business would need to be in for that to occur.

Equally, for a large PLC, it may be that your shareholders require a target share price or EPS (earnings per share) figure for the next five years. I happen to think that's a poor target (see the IBM case study), but it happens all too frequently. So you will need a strategy to get there.

Having said all that, the most likely situation is a 2–3 year horizon within which to achieve the goals. Far enough away to need a strategy, close enough to make credible plans to achieve the goals.

Goals should be outcomes

Another syndrome we have observed over the years is to muddle up process milestones with outcomes (goals). A goal – in the context of strategy – needs to be a significant outcome of the strategy and its execution that delivers organisational benefit. It's no good defining an internal metric as a goal – that way, madness lies. Let's look at a real example.

When I worked on channel strategy, one of the key requirements of the sales team was to enter each quarter's sales period with enough pipeline to make the revenue (or signings) target by the end of that quarter. Not surprisingly, this is an important prerequisite for a sales process that might have a sell cycle of 120 days. (Sell cycle is the time taken, on average, from registering a sales opportunity in the CRM system to closing it as won, lost, or postponed.) In this environment, if you don't have enough pipeline on day 1 of the quarter, then it's very hard to make up the gap, given that, on average, it takes 120 days to sell an opportunity. Let's say that for every deal that is won, two more are needed in the pipeline: a 33% win rate.

It became a major focus, therefore, to build the right amount of pipeline ready for the start of the quarter. Nothing wrong so far... but what went wrong was that pipeline then became a goal in its own right, with as much management attention as winning deals. So when a sales target was missed, the temptation was to say that there was not enough pipeline and increase the pipeline target for future quarters. Let's look at the impact of setting a pipeline target of 4x – instead of needing three opportunities at the start of the quarter, four is now the target. Immediately, as a consequence of this change, more attention is spent on driving yet more pipeline; sales directors and then sales managers are put under pressure to show actions to deliver more pipeline, and marketing faces calls to become more productive. Inevitably, the quality of the pipeline drops. There is a risk that an emailed customer request to have a phone call could be counted as a qualified opportunity, with a 'known' value of the potential sale – all before a sales rep talks to the client!

Thus, a vicious circle is created in which the poor-quality pipeline creates another miss of the quarterly target; more pipeline pressure is applied, pipeline targets become higher and higher. An extreme version of this problem could end up with pipeline targets larger than the entire market for that product set – including all competitors!

The key learning here is that pipeline, while important, is a means to an end: won opportunities (revenue/signings). The latter is the right goal.

This is why I strongly recommend focusing on outcomes, not internal process metrics, as the right kind of goals for strategies.

As a footnote, it's entirely appropriate to understand what in-process measurements should be used to determine whether each process step is doing what it is meant to do – just don't confuse those measurements with outcomes.

Goals for BAU v goals requiring a strategy change

Let's look at an example. In a commercial organisation, you have been given the goals of increasing revenue by 3% pa for the next three years and reducing costs by 2% pa over that period. When you look at the historical results for the last five years, you see that your organisation has increased revenue by 2.5% annually and reduced costs by 2% pa over those five years. Your task, therefore, is to work out how to squeeze an extra 0.5% annual revenue growth while maintaining the cost-cutting profile that you have managed for five years. Another way to look at this is that your organisation has delivered a 4.6% annual productivity improvement over the last five years, and your task is to turn that into 5.1%. Unless there is something extraordinary predicted in the external market, your strategy will be essentially similar to what you are already doing, finding a small tweak to the marketing and sales approach to deliver a slightly larger than usual increase in sales for a slightly smaller cost base.

However, if your market intelligence tells you that the market for this offering is expected to halve in the next three years, that would tell you that it is very unlikely your approach is going to deliver the objectives. This would mean you would have to more than double your market share. Doing what you are doing today is very unlikely to do that.

Similarly, if the market is expected to double over that period, I would suggest you need to discuss whether the goals are adequate. Just doing the maths tells us that if you start with a 10% market share, at the end of the three years – having achieved your goals – you will end up with a share of 5.1% and be in danger of being seen as becoming irrelevant as a player in that market.

In essence, there is a tipping point at which you recognise that the current approach, no matter how well refined and executed, cannot meet the goals – or a realisation that the goals are inadequate for the situation you are in. In the first case, you must be prepared to throw out your existing thinking and start from scratch. In the second, you must signal that your organisation needs more ambitious goals. It's not enough to take the goals you are set at face value.

How many goals?

It may be sensible to have just one, such as share price, or becoming a £10m revenue company, or being the most influential (which itself would need definition) charity in the sector. However, in a complex organisation, a single target can lead to a very one-dimensional strategy where long(er)-term or broader considerations are discarded in the pursuit of that single goal. As we saw, when IBM took on a goal to be a $20 EPS company by the end of 2015, this led to a very single-minded approach that did more damage than good. Certainly, the target was abandoned by a new CEO when it was seen to be unachievable without risking terminal damage to the company.

A single goal for an organisation risks a very unbalanced plan, where every resource is devoted to that one objective. The company needs balance to manage between short and long-term requirements and to be able to satisfy multiple stakeholders. This alone should suggest that multiple goals are going to be needed.

If there is only one target for an organisational strategy, then the only 'protective' or balancing factors you have are the organisation's mission and purpose, complemented by the values. There will almost certainly be conflict between that single goal and the values, which is unlikely to bode well for the employees and customers or service users.

Having said that, there are some plans that need to be made for what I shall refer to as 'projects'. An example would be Ofgem's strategy to enable the UK to get to net zero emissions by 2050 on its energy use. Their one page summary of the strategy is shown in Figure 25 as an example in the chapter on communications.

In the case of such projects, there is a single overarching goal, almost always with a high degree of complexity and a lengthy timescale. Setting a strategy, in this case, will be challenging, as there are few things we know with certainty about the future and looking 30 years out (as in the Ofgem example), the only thing that we can be confident of is that much will have changed.

So one goal is not enough for a 'non-project' strategy. Are ten too many? Again – almost certainly. This is because a strategy has to be simple enough to be communicated and executed, and trying to meet ten goals – some of which are almost bound to conflict with each other – is going to be unmanageable.

In practice, most strategies are designed to meet between three and six goals. This is enough to balance the approaches, make sensible trade-offs and create an explicable plan.

Making goals consistent

In many cases, strategies are written for a division or function within an organisation. It makes sense, therefore, for the goals set in those strategies to be consistent *within* the organisation and *between* other areas. What do I mean by that?

Let's take an example of a function within a large organisation – say, the HR discipline of an international company. It is unlikely that the company's goals will be appropriate for HR without modification. For example, growing market share from 10% to 20% in Europe would not be an appropriate goal for an HR function. But the Head of HR should be thinking about what his or her part of the company can do to support that goal. Therefore, all of the goals defined for HR should be linked back to the company's own objectives. For example, it may be a goal to set up new offices and recruit the best sellers from competitors in the UK, Germany, France and Italy; or perhaps to provide new training capabilities for the existing workforce. The important thing is to be able to offer complete clarity to the rest of the organisation on how your goals support the broader objectives.

That's the 'within' part of the consistency. The 'between' part relates to how the goals match up with peer parts of the company. Defining a goal to set up new offices and hire into them may not look too clever if your sales colleague is building a plan to sell over the web, supported by a lot of digital marketing and offshore telephone sales. So – as with any organisation – talk to your colleagues and make sure you have their confidence and can be consistent with their plans. Strategy reviews, as part of the strategy creation process, are put in place to catch exactly this kind of cross-functional synergy or lack of it.

Explaining the goals

When you lay out the goals in the strategy, it's important that they have a context to show *why* you have chosen those goals and set them at the levels you have. If you haven't chosen and defined the goals, it's still important to explain why they are the right ones.

In most cases, there are many different goals that could be chosen. For example, if you want to have a financial metric – and many strategies do – then there is a wide choice:

- Revenue.
- Profit.
- Expense.
- Earnings per share (EPS).
- Share price.
- …and no doubt others that are important to your particular organisation.

When you come to get sign-off for your strategy, or when you communicate it more widely, it's very helpful for people to understand why you have chosen, for example, revenue instead of EPS. The second element is to explain the magnitude of the target. In the *Goals for BAU v goals requiring a strategy change* example, the goal is the same: 3% revenue growth. However, the environment in the two examples is very different. In one case, the market for that product is forecast to shrink by 50%, and so there is a need to explain why the target of 3% growth makes sense.

Therefore, it is the section of the strategy that looks at the environment in which you are operating where you provide the narrative and justification for the targets, explaining the selection of which goals to use and what magnitude or figure is chosen.

Examples

I like to look at some real examples of goals – several are listed here:

From a charity:

"Double our charitable impact by the end of 2023."

Specific: yes.

Measurable: yes (there are accepted methodologies to do this).

Attainable: yes, the charity knows how it could achieve this.

Realistic: yes, very much in line with the charity's ethos and approach.

Time-bound: yes.

So, pretty good. From the same charity:

"Nurture our people, evolving skills as required to deliver the strategy."

Specific: no. What does 'nurture' mean? What does 'evolving skills' mean?

Measurable: no, as the words are so vague, it's impossible to have unambiguous metrics.

Attainable: yes, only because success can be claimed at any time.

Realistic: ditto.

Time-bound: no.

That was an example of a weak goal. A strategy that uses this goal as a start point could include almost any HR-related action and claim that the strategy would lead to the achievement of the goal.

Case Study: The Australian government's energy strategy

In May 2020, the Australian government published a 'Technology Investment Roadmap Discussion Paper' relating to its energy policy. It is, in practice, a draft strategy. It was published in June 2020.[25] Sections are reproduced here under the Creative Commons Attribution 4.0 International Licence: *Technology Roadmap Discussion Paper, Australian Government Department of Industry, Science, Energy and Resources.*

Before looking at a small part of it in detail, it is worth noting that the Australian government has had a troubled relationship, over several years, with its climate policy, with the ruling coalition struggling to balance support for fossil fuels – on which a large part of its exports is built – with the need to reduce emissions in the fight against climate change.

First of all, let's take a look at the vision they put forward:

"Our technology vision is for Australia to have reliable, secure and affordable energy to power the domestic economy, and economy-wide technologies deployed to maximise the employment and growth opportunities of the global shift towards lower emissions. In that vision, industry, investors, researchers, governments and the broader community will realise a lasting partnership that:

- *Develops and deploys cutting-edge technologies consistently to boost productivity.*

- *Builds on Australia's comparative advantages to create new export-facing growth and employment opportunities in emerging lower emissions industries while being cognisant of where those opportunities can benefit regional communities.*

- *Secures our place as a global low emissions technology leader by attracting and retaining the best minds in priority low emissions technology research fields and disseminating that expertise through industry to create a globally competitive workforce."*

When we take a closer look at this set of statements: nowhere does this vision say that this is about Australia becoming a low (or zero) emission country. There is plenty about developing low-emissions technology, but no mention of using it.

Saying that Australia will have reliable, secure and affordable energy is code for saying that they will stick with fossil fuels, which the federal government wants to sell as having those characteristics. Renewable energy, such as wind and solar, is intermittent, which detractors suggest is the same as unreliability. Likewise, coal is promoted as being secure and affordable.

Saying that the country has a vision for affordable and reliable electricity is hardly a vision. Most countries would regard this as basic housekeeping.

This vision is not a compelling one that would motivate the country or even those working in the energy industry.

Now let's take a look at the goals:

"The government's technology investments will drive the realisation of that vision by pursuing the following overarching goals:

- *Improving affordability of energy for Australian households and businesses.*
- *Maintaining security and reliability of energy supply.*

- *Meeting, and where possible, beating Australia's emissions reduction commitments and helping other countries to lower their emissions through the export of low emissions technologies, products and services.*

- *Seeking employment and growth opportunities, particularly in regional areas, arising from increasing global demand for low emissions energy and products.*

- *Improving affordability of energy for Australian households and businesses."*

This is very vague. If they had meant that prices would be lower, they would have said that. Improved affordability could be achieved by energy-saving measures that means industry and domestic consumers use less energy. They could meet this target by reducing taxes on fuels or by subsidising electricity and gas.

"Maintaining security and reliability of energy supply."

As the existing figures for security and reliability are not stated, it could be that the current standards are not improved. If those standards are poor, then maintaining a poor performance is hardly an impressive target. This should not be a goal anyway – it should be an undisputed ground rule to which any new technologies should adhere.

"Meeting, and where possible, beating Australia's emissions reduction commitments and helping other countries to lower their emissions through the export of low emissions technologies, products and services."

Australia's emission reduction commitments are some of the least ambitious in the world. Their promise to the world enshrined in the Paris accord of 2015 was to reduce greenhouse gas emissions by 26 to 28 per cent below 2005 levels by 2030.[26] 'Low emissions technologies' are not defined in the objectives and could just mean lower than the current technology (opening the way for natural gas).

"Seeking employment and growth opportunities, particularly in regional areas, arising from increasing global demand for low emissions energy and products."

No numbers are provided for employment or growth. No dates. No specific regions mentioned. This is so vague it would allow investment – whether small or large – in almost any technology. In a way, this is not surprising given the Australian Federal Government's notorious attitude to climate change. In the 2021 edition of the Sustainable Development Report, Australia's score for 'climate action' saw it rank last out of 177 countries assessed.[26]

Learnings:

This vision and set of targets are so loosely worded that there is almost infinite scope to return and claim success, no matter what the outcome. If, as a government policy, there is an intention to give as much scope as possible to support fossil fuels (which are major exports for Australia), then this wording makes sense. But as a strategy document, it falls well short at the very first hurdle.

As a writer of strategies, you should avoid building goals that are not smart. As a reviewer of strategies, you need to be on the alert for vague, misleading or nice-sounding objectives that are open to later – different – interpretation. Words matter, and if they are deliberately used to leave things open to later interpretation, you need to point this out.

Can you build goals from the strategy?

If you are building a situational strategy and have as good an understanding as possible of the environment, the organisational capabilities and the strategic intent that you will adopt, then yes, you can – and must – define the goals based on the last of these. However, most of the strategies that are written in organisations don't start with the situation; they are to meet assigned targets. Goals provide clarity, as long as they are well defined, about where you are aiming to go. The strategy is then about how to achieve those goals.

If you do create a strategy and then define the goals, be careful to avoid these potential issues:

- Defining goals after deciding the specific actions will almost always lead to less testing goals than would be set otherwise. In most cases, you'll be thinking about what is achievable rather than what HAS to be achieved.

- It is possible that the most difficult challenges of tough goals would be avoided, and therefore some of the reasons to think very differently ('out of the box') are lost.

- Having a direction is all very well, but it won't – on its own – force you to face the uncomfortable reality that needs a big change in the 'how' part of the strategy.

- In my experience, the main reason for deciding on strategic actions before the goals is to justify either a continuation of existing work/plans or to support a strongly held opinion by a leader, where the strategic actions and goals are subordinated to the leader's 'gut feel'. If the gut feel is justified, it would not hurt to do the work properly and define the strategy properly, as the rest of this book explains.

There is a representation of the relationship between situational and goal-based strategies, and when the goals figure in the process in Figure 3, *The relationship between strategy types and goals*. This is not a definitive picture but helps to understand when and where the goals fit into the strategy sequence. The terms 'strategic analysis', 'strategic intent' and 'strategic actions' are defined and explained in later chapters.

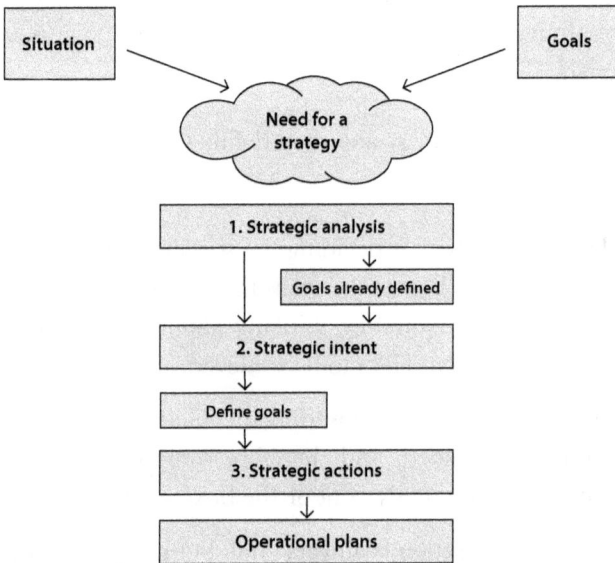

Figure 3. The relationship between strategy types and goals.

In summary, it is clear that there is an intimate relationship between the nature of the goals your strategy has to deliver and the nature of that strategy. This is hardly a surprise, but the interesting element is how the goals can force a completely different strategy.

Case Study – organisation with divisional structure

Talking to a divisional managing director who had worked in a £500m organisation working internationally, I was interested to hear his views about how the CEO had gone about setting and implementing strategy.

He told me:

During my time leading one of the divisions, a new Group CEO was recruited. During the interviews, he set out several goals for the organisation, which came across as visionary and aspirational. There were three goals, all at high level, which struck a chord with the interview panels and the recruiters. Talking to him later, he explained that he had worked with a strategy coach for the recruitment process. This was a good move, and he came across as credible and with clear thinking about the future direction of the company. He was duly hired and started to communicate the three goals he had presented at the interview.

The good news about the strategy was that it was soon nicely documented, with a reasonable number of highly polished PowerPoint slides. The bad news was that there was no information about how the three goals were to be achieved, or by when.

The three goals were:

- Impact: increase the number of customers by a factor of about ten times.

- Employee engagement: be recognised as a top employer in the sector.

- Financial: triple revenue and double net profit.

There were lots of workshops set up to get senior leaders together to brainstorm ideas, but no clear roadmap was developed as to how the organisation was going to reach these ill-defined objectives, nor was there a clear timeline.

The CEO had previously worked in the public sector and felt that the culture should almost be completely free; in practice, this meant that everyone went in different directions, with no strategic intent. He held a lot of meetings, but the cultural approach that he preferred led to an unwillingness to take decisions or give direction.

When asked for his one-line summary, he would say it was to grow the business, make more money and digitise the company. It was never really clear whether the employee engagement goal had changed to become digital transformation or whether the latter was a fourth objective. This didn't help, either.

His aspiration was to create a culture along the lines of Google or Apple. As far as strategy was concerned, though, this left a vacuum of indecision – from the top. The nice PowerPoint slides were all we had, without specific metrics or deadlines. We couldn't make anything of it. External consultants were brought in – which of course, did nothing for the morale of the leadership team – but the results were no different, as none of the stumbling blocks in the way of good strategy work had been removed.

The strategy, such as it was, never ended up being communicated to the whole organisation, as no one ever agreed on the key points, which led to divisions making up their own – disconnected – strategies.

The impact was obvious. I became so frustrated that I left about three years ago. There is only one member of the original executive team left on the board, the others having resigned as well. The impression given by the CEO is that he has little interest in the organisation or its purpose, which is a disastrous perception to propagate. Talking to my former colleagues, it seems that little has changed in the time since I left. Employee morale has plummeted, and no progress has been made on revenue or profit growth. The objectives still don't have timelines!

Learnings:

This is perhaps an unusually poor example of strategy setting, but many elements of the conversation will have echoes for readers, I am sure. This is clearly a charismatic leader who can convince a board that he is the right person for the job and has a strategic vision.

However, turning that vision into reality was beyond the individual. I suspect that if we examined the foundations on which the strategy was constructed, we would find that the understanding of the organisation's purpose and mission was missing or weak; that the vision was disconnected from them both – and from reality. There was a mismatch between the CEO's approach and the culture of the organisation he was leading. There was no strategic intent for the strategy, and no strategic actions... and most glaringly, the goals were not SMART. These sound like easy mistakes to avoid, but most leaders will have made at least some of them.

Conclusions:

Every strategy needs SMART goals. The goals may be the reason for writing the strategy, or they may come from the situation that you are in, where the strategy is the response to that situation. Goals should always be outcomes, not internal process measurements. When building a situational strategy, make sure your goals are bold enough to drive the necessary innovation.

It is not, in the end, important whether goals come before strategic actions or vice versa. What is vital is to show the clear linkage to the strategic analysis and overall strategy.

Tests for your strategy:

1. Are your goals SMART?

2. Have you distinguished between in-process measurements and real outcomes?

3. Do your goals relate precisely to each major element of the strategy?

4. Are your goals sufficiently ambitious to deliver the intent of the strategy?

5. Will your goals drive business as usual behaviour or the kind of change that is needed?

CHAPTER 4

The Essence of a Strategy: Strategic Analysis

"Good strategies start with massive amounts of quantitative analysis, hard, difficult analysis that is blended with wisdom, insight and risk-taking. Truly great companies lay out strategies that are believable and executable. Good strategies are long on detail and short on vision."

Lou Gerstner (former chair and CEO of IBM)

By the time you get to this point, you should have a very clear idea about what you need to achieve and why. If this is a situational strategy, it's being driven by the circumstances relating to the organisation. If goal-driven, then you have a set of goals to achieve.

This chapter, together with the next two, is where I am not going to tell you what your strategy should look like. For that, there are many wonderful books, some of which are listed in the bibliography.

Instead, I'm going to use this section to work through how to think about the elements of the strategy to come up with something that you and the rest of the organisation have confidence in.

There are three key elements to a strategy:

1. The why: a **strategic analysis** or diagnosis of the current and expected situation.

2. The what: a statement of **strategic intent**.

3. The how: the **strategic actions** to be taken to deliver the strategic intent.

The strategic analysis provides a compelling set of reasons for action (and later, also helps define the purpose or cause that underpins your communication plan). The strategic intent sets out what you are going to do in response to your understanding of the situation. The action plan builds a small number of key actions that are the methods you will use to meet the objectives set out in the intent.

We'll use this model to provide the shape for this chapter and the next two.

The strategic analysis ('Why')

"When your headlights aren't on, the best rearview mirror available isn't likely to improve your driving."

Dr Martha Rogers (Author, consultant)

There are two basic steps to building a good analysis for a strategy. The first is to have a really clear picture of where you are at the moment (the 'rearview mirror'). The second is to build a view of what is going to happen to the world in which you operate over the timescale of your strategy ('the headlights'). Getting these two things right – and they are difficult to do well – will enable you to make the best possible choices in your strategy. After all, it's tough to choose a direction if you don't know where you are, what's going on around you and what you want to do.

In some ways, an analysis can be easy to do; in others, it is extremely difficult. It's certainly rare – in my experience – to see it done well. If this were a medical examination, your doctor would take some time to listen to you to find out what symptoms have prompted your visit. Sometimes the diagnosis is straightforward based on what you have said. If it's less clear, the doctor may make a physical examination to find out more information about what is troubling you. Perhaps this may involve a blood test or measuring your temperature or blood pressure. You may even need to visit a hospital for an X-ray or a scan to come up with a firm diagnosis.

In any case, simple or complex, the doctor is not going to prescribe a course of treatment without being confident that there is a good determination of the illness. In very hard cases, a specialist opinion may be sought, along with more tests. Once the illness is identified, the doctor(s) will know what they can do to treat and – we hope – cure your ailment.

In the same way, our strategic analysis needs to establish exactly what needs to be done. This sounds easy enough, so why is it often done so poorly? It is frequently performed by form filling without sufficient thought. It's treated as a data gathering exercise, but the data is not turned into information and is no way to determine the best course of action.

This is the part of the process where you need data and facts to inform your decision-making. To use a well-worn army phrase, 'time spent on reconnaissance is never wasted'. Within the time limits you have, explore as much data about your customers, your business partners, your suppliers, your locations, your employees, your structure and business practices. What's gone well in the last 12-24 months, and what's gone badly? Work out why. Gather as much data as you can, and then spend quality time extracting information from that data. You will be amazed at what it can tell you if you study it.

Do be very careful about making assumptions, though. A friend told me about how he helped launch a new service in the Middle East. They had not understood the market they wanted to enter and were going to launch the service for four days a week, i.e. a Monday to Thursday offer when the working week is Sunday to Thursday.

Secondly, they had not understood their data and had assumed as people were living in the Middle East, they were from the Middle East. They jumped to the conclusion they were locals but when he researched this in detail and analysed the internal data, it became very apparent that only 15% of the customers were actually from the region, 85% were ex-pats from the UK, Europe, India, Pakistan and Africa. Had they gone ahead as planned, the outcome would have been less than happy.

Here's a case study that illustrates what can happen in an organisation that skips the strategic analysis stage and tries to create a strategic intent and strategic actions without any sense of internal or external influences and capabilities.

Case Study: Accountants

How would a small-medium regional partner-based company work on their strategy? I'm going to look at an accountancy firm based in the north east of the UK, where an old friend of mine, Sarah, has been working for the last three years. She's an experienced accountant and has held senior roles in accountancy firms in several countries.

After arriving at this firm as an equity partner, Sarah was intrigued to see that the firm had been through several changes of strategy. Until about 2014, there had been very little movement, with everyone seemingly comfortable with their client base. It had become increasingly clear to the partners that the clients were less comfortable, and they had gradually been taking their business elsewhere, with the result that by 2014, the firm was clearly in trouble.

The first action was clearly to put out the financial fires, and with the appointment of a new managing partner, they had been able to do that well enough to give them time to look at a more strategic path forward.

There had been an agreement to modernise the business and to regain lost ground, but it was not clear how they would do that. Initially, the partners agreed that they would be bold and look to double their revenues within a three year period, but the more they looked at this goal, the more they realised that there was no rationale to underpin it: why double – why not treble? What was special about three years? How on earth would they even start to achieve this?

It became clear that far from being a strategic goal based on client needs, the local market and the firm's capabilities, it was just a piece of wishful thinking that quickly fell apart when closely examined. Rightly, this was abandoned, and the search for the right strategy was resumed. It was very clear that right across the company, there was an appetite for a clear direction and focus – but it was far from easy to work out what that should be and getting agreement from all the partners. Sarah has not seen much evidence of a concerted effort to build an insightful analysis for the firm. While there is data about clients, the regional market and competitors – both local and national – this hasn't been brought together into an accepted piece of work that would allow conclusions to prepare the thinking for an overall strategic response to what that analytic process would produce.

Not surprisingly given this, Sarah explains that to this day, there isn't a strategic direction that everyone has agreed to. There are several versions that are referred to:

- Create leaders who build teams.

- Maintain and invest in the company's strengths, improve training, succession planning and community presence.

- Build cross-company awareness to improve cross-selling of other departments' services.

What has been difficult is to find a direction that each of the eight departments will sign up to; in short, there is no shared sense of purpose that runs across the firm. The departmental heads are in charge of their fiefdoms and resent anything that appears to them as a loss of control – and, therefore, prestige. This lack of consensus is not helped by the fact that there is no strategic goal that would drive the adoption of a particular direction.

Having said that, there has been agreement on five strategic actions to underpin the growth of the firm. These are:

1. Attracting larger business clients (between 500 and 2000 employees).

2. A focus on international taxation (led by Sarah with her international accounting experience).

3. Cross-selling other departments' services.

4. Wealth planning and protection.

5. Gaining referrals from smaller accountancy firms where they have client needs outside their skill areas.

These strategic actions are not yet underpinned by clear goals or timeframes; there is no agreed set of metrics, no management system in place, and these headlines have not yet been turned into operational plans. However, work is going on to rectify these shortcomings.

The lack of a coherent overall strategic direction has impacted execution priorities, though. One year was lost to implementation of a new all-encompassing customer relationship management system that was meant to provide cross-departmental views of each client, give accurate and up-to-date information about the client's needs and preferences; show what sales and marketing activities each client had engaged with, and allow integration with the existing system for time allocation and billing. This has proved very costly, slower to implement than planned and still has not been universally adopted across the company, owing to two of the eight heads of department refusing to engage. Disappointingly, the partners agreed to a year's pause on the strategy implementation to allow for this internal exercise.

Another example was a pet project of one of the leading partners, who made a unilateral decision to invest a significant amount of resources into personal accounting services – which led to a tiny amount of business before being closed down at a very significant loss. This was not only inconsistent with the five strategic actions but diverted resources away from them, thus creating more execution delays.

Sarah's conclusions, after three years?

She feels that she is working in a business where the vast majority are committed to great client services. There is a great deal of financial and accounting expertise; there is a market ready to be opened up in that region – with a good fit to their offerings. On the other hand, politics and personalities are preventing a united strategy; leadership can be by whim rather than through logic and planning; and execution is held up by siloed departments who sit uneasily together, rather than working in true partnership for the benefit of the firm overall.

Learnings:

Talent and enthusiasm are not enough. These things need to be marshalled and brought together under the umbrella of an overarching strategy. Without a credible analysis process, it's incredibly difficult to create a strategic intent; it's even harder to justify why one particular direction should be selected rather than another.

The lack of strategic analysis has led to a lack of strategic intent, which, in turn, has meant that the five strategic actions lack the underpinnings of a clear rationale, compounded by the lack of SMART goals and management system for each one.

More fundamentally, the lack of shared purpose is likely to prevent the emergence of a company-wide strategy. While the baronial style of departmental leadership remains, it's hard to see how that can come about.

Is it all bad? Far from it. This is an organisation with over 20,000 business clients, seven regional offices and which remains nicely profitable. It contains very capable and professional accountants and has some very capable leaders. It is not going to get into deep trouble – at least not quickly. But it is far from fulfilling its potential until it can get to grips with its purpose, realise that there are cultural issues to fix, and at the same time, put in place a strategy that everyone in the organisation can sign up to.

One frequent error when performing your strategic analysis is to be the victim of confirmation bias. This means that you think you know what the data is telling you, and you pay attention, therefore, only to the data that agrees with your pre-determined conclusion. An example would be when your company is considering launching a new product line and undertakes some research to see whether the new line should be manufactured and taken to market. Bear in mind that the people sponsoring the research are very likely to be the ones emotionally invested in the idea of a new product line, and therefore, they will look for the feedback that is consistent with a continuation of the plan. Often, people will disregard information contrary to their bias on the grounds that it is – for example – anecdotal while eagerly seizing on equally anecdotal data that supports the idea. The larger the financial and emotional investment, the more likely people are to disregard contrary information. The definitive guide to this bias can be found in *Thinking Fast and Slow* by Daniel Kahneman.

To gather and analyse a lot of data is good – but not enough. The leadership team has to have minds that are sufficiently open to understand what information is coming out of the data.

A military example shows the risk of having a closed mind and an inability to recognise how an innovation is going to affect the organisation. After the First World War, the great military writer and historian, Basil Liddell Hart, tried to persuade the British army of the best way to use tanks in modern warfare. He submitted an essay to the army called 'Mechanisation of the Army' for a competition. The judges were a Field Marshal, a General and a Colonel. With a mindset that looked backwards rather than forwards, they rejected his essay in favour of one called 'Limitations of the Tank'. If this were the only consequence, it would be lamentable, but much worse was the fact that the German army staff were avid readers of Liddell Hart's work and exploited it to great advantage in the Second World War. So even when the right information is presented to people, it does not always mean that they will recognise its importance, let alone do something about it.

Lots of data is very helpful as you go through the strategic analysis stage, but you can't (OK, you shouldn't) put a spreadsheet into the strategy. Not even a small one. This discipline requires you to present what are often complex topics succinctly and turn huge amounts of data into digestible pieces of information.

Next, let's look at a case study that shows what can be done when an opportunity is spotted, and a great deal of work goes into the strategic analysis stage, enabling a very successful strategy for a start-up.

Case study: Club Together

This case study is a little unusual because we get to look at a company from the first idea of the founder through to its closure. It's a success story, but with the caveat that there are some things that the best strategy can't control. I spoke at some length with the founder and chief executive, Mike, who told me a fascinating story.

Club Together was the offshoot of a major pensions administration organisation with two parent companies that delivered complex pension administration and payment solutions to 2,000 clients in the UK, including 50% of the FTSE100. Their services were provided for 2.9 million pensioners across more than 700 schemes and over 100 clients in the public and private sectors.

Mike was working in one of the parent companies as market development director, with a brief to create new products and offerings and to find new or adjacent markets for expansion. One of the key performance indicators (KPIs) for the parent company was the number of people being paid a pension each month, which created a moment of insight: the millions of pensioners were an opportunity for new services and a new approach.

One of the best strategic insights that can be gained is to look afresh at what assets your organisation really has, not necessarily what's listed on the balance sheet, and to re-imagine how those assets can be used. This case study is the story of how that was achieved in one company.

Being a pensions administrator, of course, this organisation held completely accurate and up-to-date data on the recipients, such as their age, address and pension income. Mike talked to savings and investment companies to gauge their level of interest and was overwhelmed by their enthusiasm for the concept he put forward to them: being able to reach this audience to sell their products and services.

Pulling together the themes, Mike presented a concept paper to the board. The initial response from many around the table was clear: "We don't do that!" and "What about data protection?" Without the CEO's intervention, the paper would have been quickly written off, but fortunately, he (the CEO) could see the potential in the idea, and he asked Mike to investigate further, on the condition that there was to be no improper use of data.

The next stage of development involved both internal and external work. Internally, the advice from the data protection officer was, 'don't do it – this will be illegal'. Mike also needed to work out the detailed business case based on the monetisation of the data – assuming that a legal way to do this could be found. The legal question was finally resolved by bringing in advice from a legal firm with specialist knowledge about data management and use. They advised that – with the right approach and permissions – the data could be used for the intended purpose.

The internal business case revolved around the commission that service providers would pay to Club Together (the name that was settled on for this new organisation) for introducing their products to their target audience.

Externally, the case had to be made first to the pension clients, as it would be their approval that would be needed even to get started. Mike made many presentations to the trustees of the various pension schemes, and it quickly became apparent that there could be a beneficial exchange of value. Pension schemes are obliged, by law, to provide annual communications – as a minimum – to their pensioners. By including the scheme communications with Club Together communications, considerable costs could be saved for them. The potentially beneficial offers that could be made to the pensioners was also a powerful case for the trustees who could be seen as adding more value than simply providing a pension. Trustees were reassured that everything would be done without any legal exposure and that all communications would be entirely above board.

With those approvals coming in, Club Together was in a position to approach the various companies involved in (for example) insurance, tourism, holidays, furnishings, house adaptation, investments etc. By bringing together such a potentially enormous target market, with the knowledge of accurate targeting because of the very high quality of the data, there was a very strong case to be made for these companies to engage. There was – as predicted – an enthusiastic response, and all were expected to create special offers unique to this route to market on this basis.

Focus group research with representative members of the audience, however, provided some insights that Mike describes as 'earth shattering' – mainly that not one of the people receiving pensions realised that the company performing the administration was involved in their pension at all. The pensioners all thought they were dealing with the pension scheme of their previous employers. This revelation meant that the communication package should be branded not, as expected, from the administrator but from the pension scheme.

The next step – and this turned out to be a genuine inspiration – was to involve the pensioners themselves in the selection and promotion of the products being offered through regular communications. The pensioners devised criteria to evaluate and select potential offers and would then score the offers. Only the ones that passed a fairly high-quality bar would then be selected. Regional focus groups were held quarterly, using a nice hotel and a free buffet lunch. There were typically 12 to 15 participants and partners. The pensioners received a small payment for their time. It was a short day – between 11:00 and 15:00 with the morning session covering communications: what they liked, what they didn't like and what could improve. In the afternoon, they reviewed products, discussing what they wanted, their experiences, who they currently used, their likes and dislikes, which companies they considered good and bad, and what an ideal product would look like.

The process quickly became well established around a formula that proved highly successful, using what Club Together called the '3 Rs'.

1. Research

   What do members want a better deal on?

   Evaluate the market to find reputable companies that could offer the best deals.

   Select the best company and product and negotiate an exclusive Club Together offer.

2. Review

   Ask a Club Together member to review the offer from a member's point of view.

Particular attention paid to honesty, price, service, information and recognition.

Score the product out of 25.

3. Recommend

After thorough research and review and when the member and Club Together are happy, the product is offered to all Club Together members.

The marketing, in turn, featured pensioners strongly, as recommendations from their peer group proved very powerful. When the direct mail communication landed with the pensioners, there was an extraordinarily high open rate, based on the previous employer's name and the fact that the offers included were highly relevant and featured people from a similar background.

The value proposition for the pensioners was clearly defined as a programme for pension scheme retirees with communication via direct mail, magazine, email and website, with:

• Preferential and exclusive offers.

• Information and advice.

• A sense of community.

• Opportunity to boost your pension.

• Participation in the Club Panel.

• Free to the scheme and pensioner.

One of the most successful areas was around the utilities market and how to switch providers. This led on to the introduction of a company called Utility Warehouse, which acts as an aggregator for utilities. This had huge take-up.

Interestingly, Club Together was run on an outsourced model, which meant that only four employees were needed. The mailing house, printing, and marketing were all outsourced, providing great flexibility and low costs.

Once the concept was proven, this opened up new possibilities by taking the offer to other organisations who used different pension administrators or who administered their own pensions, which proved to be another valuable source of revenue.

So, what happened to Club Together?

The parent companies made decisions to focus on core activities and didn't see this (despite being an excellent sales tool) as right for their portfolio and tried to sell it off via a joint venture. When they couldn't find a buyer, it was closed down, despite being profitable from very early days right the way through to closure. It is possible that this came about from the parent companies not having a clear idea of their purpose – although tough decisions are often made for the opposite reason. We shall never know.

There we have it – a cradle to grave story about a successful company with a strategy that worked, and yet it still folded for reasons beyond its control.

Learnings:

This situation is at least partly a 'blue ocean' strategy, as Mike found complementary product and service offerings and understood the emotional appeal to buyers of products selected and recommended by their peers. There wasn't anything else in the market like that at the time – and there hasn't been a significant replication of the model that either Mike or I are aware of – although the GDPR regulations have since changed the landscape somewhat.

In our terms, this was a situational strategy: where a perspicacious leader spotted a real gap in the market and built a mechanism to supply that gap. The strategic intent was to use the unique data asset owned by the company to deliver value to pensioners. The goals – and Mike was unequivocal that SMART goals were an essential part of his strategy – came once the strategic intent was defined.

Get the strategic analysis right: this was done very well. With the CEO as a committed supporter, Mike had the approval he needed to get going, and by delivering results, he brought the rest of the executive team on board. One of the elements of real quality in the strategic analysis was to involve the target audience right from the start and then regularly throughout the implementation. The insights from the pensioners provided actionable information that would have been difficult or impossible to obtain any other way, which meant that every step in the plan was founded on a deep understanding of the values, wants and needs of those being targeted.

What started out as a very difficult birth (in one meeting the in-house data protection officer stood up with their hand out and said: "Halt – this is illegal.") ended up as a very successful enterprise until it was closed. Mike's story was that he moved on to roles as chair and non-executive director of various enterprises. His experience did him no harm!

Where can you find helpful data?

1. Listen to the customer.

This is always a good thing to do, as in the last case study. Getting a true and representative set of data to tell you what existing and potential customers think is incredibly important. You can use client complaints and compliments as a source of helpful data. Take time to talk to them at conferences and events. Get a feel for their views on the market – what's changing, what attracts their attention and why. What do they think of your competitors? Are there new entrants trying to make inroads into your market share that you haven't come across yet? Will they spend more money on your category of offering next year or less, and why? What do they think about your products and services? Do your employees come across well? There's a goldmine of information in there.

However, don't think you will get a strategic prescription from your clients. Many of them will offer you opinions about what you should do and how you should do it, but you need to decide how much weight you attach to these suggestions. Mostly your customers will know much more about themselves (and/or their businesses) than they know about your organisation. I have a wonderful cartoon from many years ago showing a strategy brainstorming session, in which the participants all agree that what customers want is 'better products, for free', and conclude that they will sell what they have and call it a strategy. I'm not that cynical.

2. Use Market data.

This often concerns people a lot. You may be able to obtain market data from your internal market intelligence team (if you work in a large enough company) or perhaps from a consultancy or market data service you subscribe to. Some industries may be highly regulated, and the regulatory body produces a lot of information.

If the information is available to everyone, you might think that it's hard to gain competitive advantage from it, and you'd be right. But that's not an excuse for not looking hard at the data to extract insights that are helpful to your organisation.

It's quite possible that you work in an industry sector where there is precious little information readily available from any source. That's not an excuse for throwing up your hands and guessing. Anything here is going to be helpful. The annual reports of your competitors, especially if they are listed companies, often provide useful detail. Social media postings from your competitors or target customers. Local and national newspapers. Your own sales force, distributors, resellers, retailers. Your accountants, your marketing agency, your business partners. Talk to your non-executive directors. Any one of these sources may only contribute a small part of the puzzle, but the more pieces you can find, the more a picture will emerge. Don't be afraid to make estimates. Almost every piece of market data I have ever seen is an estimate. The best market data are a set of very well-informed estimates.

Using market data in your strategy brings its own set of presentational issues. The big problem is that everyone knows that in almost every case, it's not accurate. As for market growth projections, we all know that they are going to be wrong – a bit or a lot. That's the only thing we do know!

Having said that, if you have satisfied yourself that you have the best available information, that it's been sense-checked and that it's consistent with what you do know, then use the data. If you're challenged on the data by a reviewer/approver, you can be confident that you don't have a better source of information. Remember that if you've done a good job on this, then *they don't have a better source either.* Don't be brow-beaten into accepting 'gut feel' estimates. If the gut feel is a good source (and it may be), then you will have taken it into account already.

Once you have your information, there's a real temptation to include a lot of fancy charts just because you can. Some of these will be helpful and lead to insights, better plans and the right actions – but only if used in the right way.

Here are a couple of charts I have made up for a fictional company:

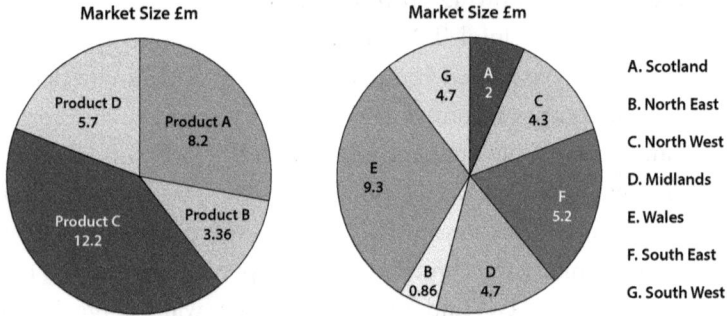

Market Size £m

Market Size £m

A. Scotland

B. North East

C. North West

D. Midlands

E. Wales

F. South East

G. South West

Figure 4. **Market size data for a fictional company.**

Perfectly nice charts, showing the size of the market for your four product ranges in the UK. They also show the market size by UK region. So what? How can you use this information?

First of all, there is more that you could use. Let's add in some market growth data.

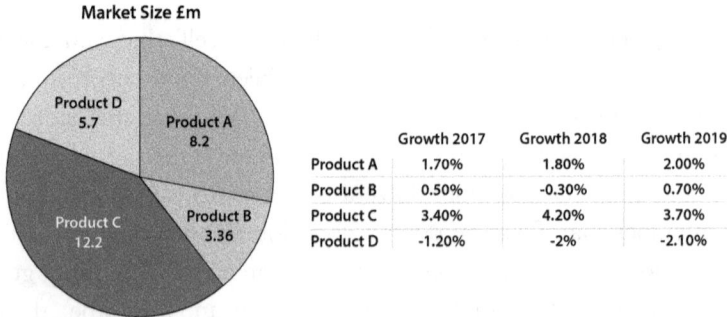

Market Size £m

	Growth 2017	Growth 2018	Growth 2019
Product A	1.70%	1.80%	2.00%
Product B	0.50%	-0.30%	0.70%
Product C	3.40%	4.20%	3.70%
Product D	-1.20%	-2%	-2.10%

Figure 5. **Market data for products with historical market growth.**

So what can we see? The biggest market has been the fastest growing. The market for Product D has been shrinking consistently. Finally, let's add in some growth projections:

Market Size £m

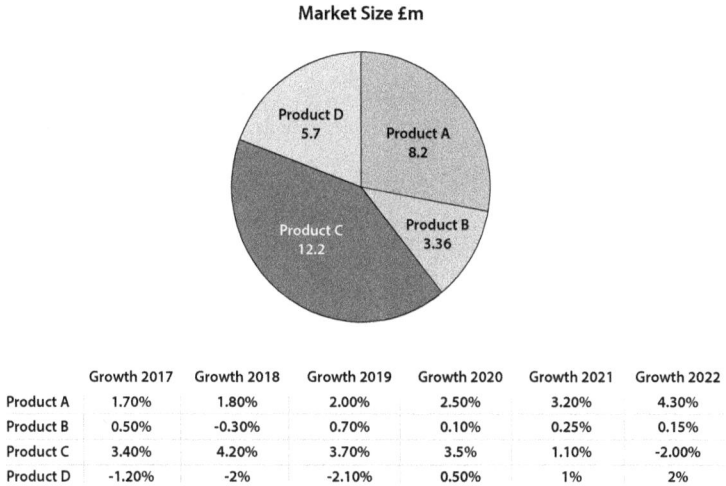

	Growth 2017	Growth 2018	Growth 2019	Growth 2020	Growth 2021	Growth 2022
Product A	1.70%	1.80%	2.00%	2.50%	3.20%	4.30%
Product B	0.50%	-0.30%	0.70%	0.10%	0.25%	0.15%
Product C	3.40%	4.20%	3.70%	3.5%	1.10%	-2.00%
Product D	-1.20%	-2%	-2.10%	0.50%	1%	2%

Figure 6. Market data with historical and projected growth.

Now things look different again. The point of producing this information is not to tell you about how to analyse this data. If you are reading this book, you know how to do that and have probably done so many times. It's to make you think about how you present it as part of your paper. Many times, I have seen strategy papers that just dump something like one of these charts on the page and move on. Explain the context, explain how you are using this information, draw clear conclusions and make the recommended action part of the narrative.

3. Talk to your employees.

Your employees are the people closest to the customer. They probably get lots of useful information every day. If you are well organised, there may be an existing mechanism to capture client feedback – other than your complaints system. Even so, talk to employees regularly. They will almost certainly make a comment that seems obvious to them but strikes you as interesting or even vital.

You probably employ people who worked for a competitor before joining you. Talk to them as soon as they join. They won't be able to share confidential information – and you shouldn't ask them to – but there is much that is not restricted that is helpful, often about the culture, attitudes and values of the competitor. It's sometimes more about adding colour to the black and white details that you already know about the competitor. It's all going to be helpful.

4. Talk to your business partners.

Your business partners almost certainly work closely with the customers in your market. They are another means of understanding what happens in the market. They also often deal with your competitors and will be forthright about what they perceive as their strengths and weaknesses.

In summary, there is usually more good quality market data available than you first believe there to be. I hope that you don't start looking for it when you have to write a strategy. It should be part of what your organisation does all the time. The strategy provides a reason to pull it all together and look at it with fresh eyes to help get the big picture in place for your work.

The analytical tools

There are some very good tools that can be used to help in performing this work. But like any tool, they can be misused. Possibly the worst abused tool in the kit is the poor old SWOT chart. I bet you've seen a lot of these. You may have constructed quite a few. And what happened to the information that you put on there?

Precisely.

It ended up as a page in the deck that everyone skips over. A few people may read it, nod sagely and move on. What on earth is a SWOT chart for, then? If properly used, it's a very good and powerful way to summarise these four areas: Strengths, Weaknesses, Opportunities and Threats. But the only reason for doing it is if you:

- Work out how best to apply the organisation's strengths to the actions you create as part of the strategy.

- Decide what to do about the weaknesses: have a strategy that avoids or minimises weaknesses or invests time and effort to eliminate those weaknesses.

- Decide which opportunities to exploit and which to ignore.

- Build a defence mechanism for threats that cannot be avoided; steer a course to avoid threats if that's desirable and possible.

Every time I see a SWOT chart in a strategy paper, I check to see how it has been used to inform the decisions being taken. I am usually disappointed.

The next most common is the PESTLE chart (Political, Economic, Social, Technological, Legal, Environmental). Again, these charts are populated with long lists of things that are going on under these headings, often nothing to do with the organisation. If you are going to use this (perfectly good) chart, then think about what is relevant to the organisation, what the implications are going to be, and what you need to do about each selected topic. Again, avoid clichés which just state the obvious. Under Technology, putting 'industry digital transformation' is worthless because every industry is undergoing a series of rapid changes owing to new technologies and new ways of applying established technologies. Be more precise about the digital innovations that make a difference to your company. What are they? Are they going to advantage or disadvantage you? How certain are you of the feasibility of the technology that is supposed to drive change? For example, if you work in the energy industry, you could include fusion as a future power source. But if it's not going to affect you over the timescale of the plan you are building, don't bother.

The last part of PESTLE is environmental, which is rapidly taking on more importance for almost every organisation. It may be that supply chains become stressed by increased flooding; possibly a business connected to fossil fuels becomes socially unacceptable, or the use of renewable energy is mandated by your key customers. I would not expect to see any organisational strategy that did not look at the potential impacts of climate change and the environment.

A well-known tool for strategy, devised by Michael Porter as far back as 1980, is the five forces model to determine pressures in a particular industry. The five forces are:

- Threat of new entrants.
- Bargaining power of suppliers.
- Bargaining power of buyers.
- Threat of substitute products or services.
- Industry competitors.

These five forces determine how intense the competition is – and is likely to be – in an industry and also gives a view about how profitable that industry is likely to be. The model has been very effective over several decades in helping determine the strategic decisions that need to be made across all the forces that affect competition (or 'extended rivalry', as Porter puts it) and profitability.

A case study contributor pointed out to me that the thinking in too many organisations is overly focused on internal issues and that a rigorous understanding of the competition is essential for commercial companies.

I have mentioned this model not to give a full explanation of how it works but to remind you that it is a very powerful addition to the analysis if used properly. More information about how to use it, and the context, can be found in Michael Porter's *Competitive Strategy*.

You may want to use a tool that explains why you are making some strategic choices. One way to look at this would be to assess each region's sales team's ability to sell and compare that with how attractive the market is. Again, you probably know how to do this, and if you don't, there are plenty of textbooks that will tell you how to. Therefore, you produce a chart that looks a bit like this:

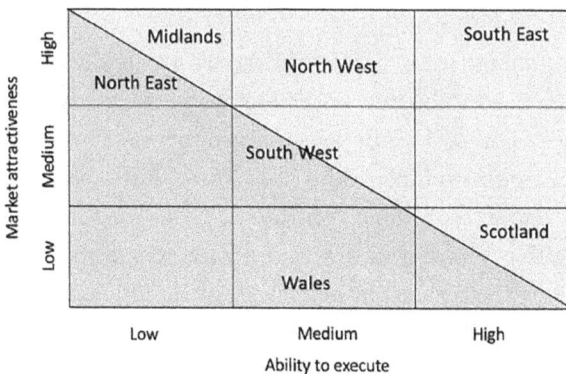

Figure 7. Market attractiveness v Ability to execute.

Briefly, the chart provides a matrix view of how attractive the market is (here, simplified to just the size; in the real world, you would include other weighted factors and score each one) against the ability of each regional team to execute; in other words, how likely it is that they will consistently make the targets. Again, this would be a score created from a number of weighted factors such as skills, experience, support, leadership etc.

The importance of this is – again – what you do with the information that it provides. In our example, Scotland is an unattractive market, but you have high confidence that the team will make their target. Make sure you invest enough to keep them on track, or at least don't cut their resources. The Midlands is a good market, but the team there scores badly on their ability to make targets. That, in itself, is not enough to make decisions. You need to know why they score badly. Only when you really understand what is going on can your plan include actions to improve the ability of the team to do what you need or to remove resources to place them where you will get a better return. Given the attractiveness of the market, you may choose the former option. A third example would be the South West – neither very attractive as a market nor particularly good at delivery. The decision is yours... but make one!

If you are going to make good decisions about the situation you are in, you also need to be able to distinguish between symptoms and root causes. This is a really important dimension to the strategic analysis. In our example, both the North East region and the Midlands region score lowly on the ability to execute. That's the symptom. To get to root causes, ask why the symptom occurs – and keep asking why to each subsequent answer until you really get to the basic issue underpinning the symptom.

Let's say that the North East region has performed badly because it is persistently under headcount. People, once recruited, keep leaving. Why? It's because the onboarding process in that region is poorly done. Why? That's because they don't have the resources to do the onboarding properly. Why? Because a decision was taken to reallocate that headcount into sales. Why? Because the regional director was struggling to make targets and prioritised more sales instead of onboarding. Now we are starting to get to the root cause.

The Midlands region, on the other hand, is up to full strength and has been for a good while. Why is their performance weak? The numbers tell you that they sell at a lower price than other regions, and the sell cycle is a month longer than anywhere else. Why? It turns out that a new competitor has started its UK operation in the Midlands and plans to expand to other regions. Accordingly, your response to the first problem in the North East is going to be totally different to the plan you build for the Midlands.

These are all basic techniques, but so often not used or poorly thought through.

One tool that was invented to find opportunities for completely new approaches to markets is the strategy canvas (Chan Kim and Mauborgne) which identifies the factors that your industry competes on and shows which of the factors you choose to prioritise. This is a very good tool for understanding your industry and giving a perspective on both your approach and the competition's. It can be used even if competing (to use their term) in the middle of the red ocean. A very simple example is shown here for a fictitious company that makes musical instruments.

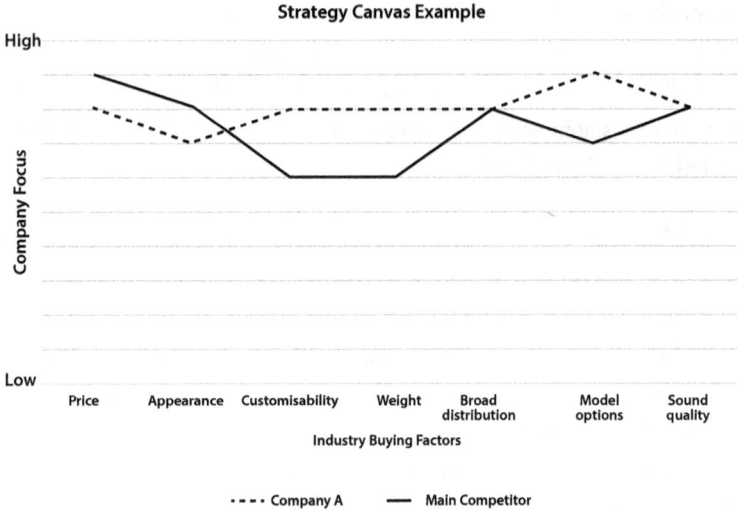

Figure 8. Strategy canvas example.

This chart shows two notional competitors selling musical instruments. The seven factors along the x axis are what buyers for those products care about. The y axis shows the emphasis placed on each factor by the two companies in their business model. It is easy to see that they do not have clearly differentiated positions, and we would expect competition between them to be tough, hand-to-hand combat on a regular basis. Let's invent a new competitor and see what happens if they take a different approach:

Strategy Canvas Example

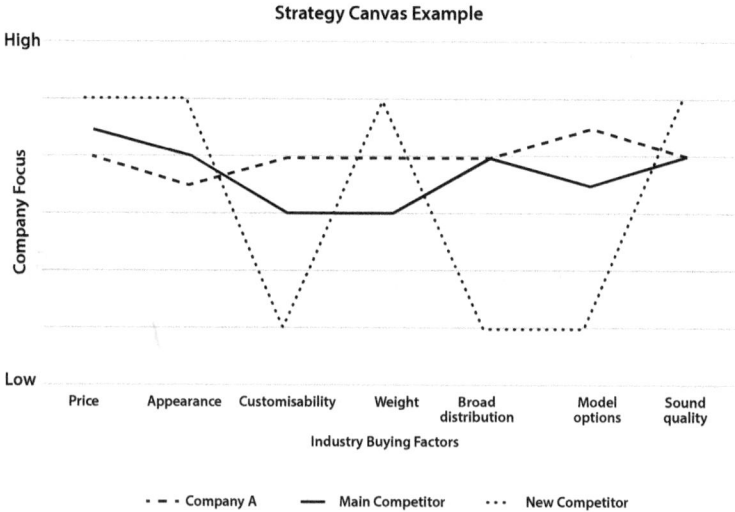

Figure 9. Strategy canvas with new competitor.

Here we can see the new competitor who has entered the market with a different approach. High price is justified by first-rate appearance, top quality sound and light weight, whereas they eliminate the need for customisation, lots of model options and the instrument is only available through high-end boutique sellers. You can see how this strategy is clearly differentiated from the two main sellers in this market, which is one of the key indicators of a good strategy.

The value of the tool, therefore, is found in the exercise to understand the buyer factors in that industry (and weighting them would be potentially useful); to see how your own approach is positioned on the canvas; to compare key competitors and finally to plot an alternative approach with a much more clearly differentiated focus on selected factors.

The strategy canvas is both a diagnostic tool and a strategy development tool. You can find many more examples of how it has been used in *Blue Ocean Strategy*.

In summary: check – and keep checking – that everything that is included in the paper is there for a reason and that it forms part of the narrative, structure or logic of the strategy. If it's just padding, get rid of it. Either delete or move to the appendices.

All these elements are part of the strategic analysis. Put in good work here, and the answers will be – if not obvious – clearer. Quite a lot of the time, your strategic analysis will come up with facts that are unpalatable or politically difficult. Your sponsor (if you are not at the top of the organisation) will be vital in keeping things on track. It's no good writing a politically sensible but dishonest strategic analysis. In the end, that just fudges the issues. If the organisation is incapable of truthful self-scrutiny, then find another company to work for, or don't worry about reading any further!

How often should you do the analysis work?

There are two problems frequently encountered with analysis.

The first is that it is treated as a one-off exercise that is done as part of the annual strategy planning cycle. Your organisation should be performing this work all the time. Customer feedback doesn't wait for your planning to begin. Market changes are happening all the time. New competitors or substitutes may need an urgent response. So, you should have this information at your fingertips whenever you perform this part of the strategy creation process, and it should be accurate and up-to-date.

The second issue in my experience is that when writing the analysis section (it may be called the 'market review' or 'environmental study' or similar), the easy thing to do is to turn to last year's plan and update it. This leads to a quicker and easier piece of work, but one that is much less valuable. Ideally, the work should be done by a new person each time, starting with a blank piece of paper.

That way, there is a better chance of new insights, fresh dimensions being provided, and old ways of thinking discarded. Keep this intellectually fresh and open. Avoid tired repetition of what people know or what they expect to hear. It is almost certain that a lot has changed since you last performed this exercise. Capture what is different and why. That is what should be informing your thoughts on the best strategic response, not a summary that is basically the same as last year and the year before.

Lastly, when writing up your strategic analysis, keep it succinct and clear. Make sure that the evidence to support your figures is included in an appendix rather than in the main body of the document. Use pictures, charts, tables and text to make the section readable. Be very clear about your conclusions. At the end of the section, the reader should know exactly what strategic analysis you have reached and why you reached it.

Conclusions:

Quality strategic analysis is the key to the selection of the right strategy. It is hard to spend too much time and effort on strategic analysis as long as you continue to derive new insights from your work. Get as much quantitative and qualitative data as you can. Turn your data into information. Use the right tools in the right way to help reach a good strategic analysis. Keep it fresh – try not to recycle work from previous strategies; provide new insights. Be clear in the way you explain the strategic analysis.

Tests for your strategy:

1. Have you got every possible source of quality data lined up to mine for information?

2. Can you find a way to avoid confirmation bias as you analyse the data?

3. Where using tools like SWOT and PESTLE, are they adding to the thinking, or just there because someone thinks they should be?

4. Have you tested your findings with those closest to the market?

5. Have you laid out the information as clearly as possible?

6. Are your conclusions clear and supported by the narrative you have written?

7. Have you laid out a timeframe for refreshing the data regularly?

CHAPTER 5

The Essence of a Strategy – The Strategic Intent

"You cannot be everything to everyone. If you decide to go north, you cannot go south at the same time."

Jeroen De Flander (Strategy execution thought leader)

Now you have created a strategic analysis of the state of the organisation, the market that it serves, its competition, external factors likely to affect it, and its ability to serve its customers or service users.

Your strategic intent gives a summary view of how you will respond to the situation as outlined in your analysis. It also creates an approach to exploit the opportunities that your analysis has prioritised.

Before we work out how to decide on a strategic intent, there are a couple of concepts that are important to consider. One is the part that change must play in a good strategy, and the other is about distinguishing between business as usual (BAU) and strategy.

Change

Before starting on how to define your strategic intent, I want to look at the concept of change and how it applies to strategic thinking. This may seem obvious, but so many strategies that land on my metaphorical desk don't seem to want to introduce change as part of the strategy.

It's a given that the world around us is changing all the time. The nearer world of the industry in which our organisation operates is constantly mutating too. Your PESTLE chart – if you have done one – will have highlighted some of the most pertinent changes that will, or may, affect your company. There will be multiple dimensions of change that are important: political, regulatory, demographic, environmental, cultural, economic, and closer to home, shareholder views, competitor mergers and acquisitions, new products, suppliers going bust, customer preferences, relationships with local government and so on. Your organisation is having to change to deal with all these things and more, and for some of them, probably doing it without much conscious effort. Others pop up as a crisis or new opportunity and require senior management attention.

The logic, therefore, tells us that the environment around you is changing and that your organisation is also changing. When the two are changing at roughly the same rate, things appear to be working as usual: steady as she goes. However, consider what happens when the market moves faster than your company. For a while, it's possible to survive, but after long enough, the market realises that you are not keeping up. Your new product launches don't set the bar; they just look like imitations of what your competitors have already done. Your new service offerings don't excite, they look like 'me too' exercises. Eventually, you find you have developed an offering for a market that no longer merits the investment – or worse, has disappeared. By consistently not changing at the rate of the market, you have become irrelevant. I'm sure you can think of examples from your industry where this has happened.

There is also a risk on the other side. If you change too fast, then you may arrive at a destination in the market that your consumers have not yet reached, and then have an uncomfortable wait to see if they will adopt your new offering or whether your competition will steal them away with a more familiar-looking product or service. Rapid change can also take a toll on the organisation, particularly if the workforce can't see the point.

Figure 10, *The boundaries of change*, puts this into a graphical view. The bottom, x, axis is time and the left, y, axis is the rate of change. In this greatly simplified view, the rate of change varies historically up to the present day, shown by the solid line. After the current date, the shaded bands above and below the solid line represent the margins of change that the market will tolerate going forward. Too little and you are below the band of tolerance and have become irrelevant; too much and you go above the shaded area and lose touch with the market.

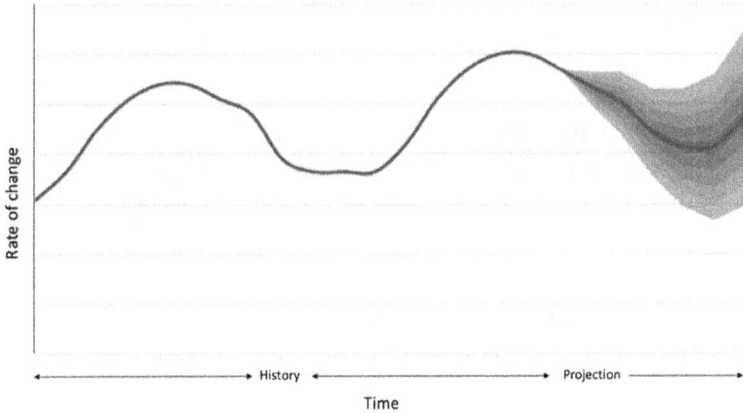

Figure 10. The boundaries of change.

The point – which I hope is obvious – is that your strategy must include elements of change that are sufficient to sustain the organisation in the environment around it. It's better to be changing slightly faster than the market rather than slightly slower. There are a couple of obvious risks in changing too fast or too slowly.

As an example, Nokia used to be the world's largest mobile phone manufacturer. In 2007 and 2008, it enjoyed sales of more than €50bn. But sales started to slide, and by 2012, they had fallen to €30bn. In 2013, the stampede happened, and sales plunged by 58% to €12.7bn.[27] The next year, Nokia sold its mobile devices business to Microsoft, and now it is a network infrastructure business.

Let's call this stampede the 'Roadrunner effect' after the cartoon character that runs over the cliff, and for a tantalising moment, keeps going before plummeting to earth.

The danger of changing faster than the market is real, too, but less frequently seen. Remember Google Glass? These revolutionary glasses were launched in April 2012 with customary hype and great expectations about how this would change peoples' lives. I remember a charity for the disabled being very excited about the potential to help blind people. The concept was great, but the execution wasn't. The glasses cost £990 in the UK, definitely not a trivial purchase.

By the end of 2014, thanks to concerns about privacy and safety, as well as some businesses and restaurants banning the use of Glass on their premises, the world had seemed to grow tired of Project Glass and the fact that it had yet to become what Google had promised. By January 2015, the project had been killed off.

I call this the 'Icarus effect' after the Greek legend who flew too close to the sun and the heat melted the wax that held his wings together. The end result is the same as the Roadrunner effect: a fall to the ground.

There's another legitimate point to consider, though. What if you genuinely create a new market? This was what W Chan Kim and Renee Mauborgne talked about in their book, *Blue Ocean Strategy*. Doesn't that make the whole concept of change redundant because it defines a space with high value and low costs that no one else can get into? 'Make the competition irrelevant'. Of course, this represents the ultimate degree of change – something entirely new. But once your blue ocean strategy is launched, you can't sit on your laurels. You've created a new market, and that, in turn, will evolve with new entrants and more competitiveness. So you will need to change as fast as the market you created changes, or you will suffer the Roadrunner or Icarus effect in due course.

There's a clear point emerging from this about the need for constant change. In a broader context, for an organisation to survive, it needs to adapt – constantly – to its environment. It's not a novel concept; Darwin came up with the concept of evolution and the survival of the fittest. It is a good parallel to draw when looking at strategy because the underlying theme of all strategies has to be change.

How good are big companies at adapting to their environments? Let's take a look at the Dow Jones index to give us an idea. The Dow Jones is an index of 30 large US companies, based on the share price with a divisor to allow for stock splits etc. It was started in 1884 with 11 companies – almost all railroad companies – and expanded to 20 companies in 1916, reaching its current format of 30 companies in 1928. I decided to see how much its composition had changed during my lifetime. As you will see from this table,[28] there is only one company, Procter and Gamble, that has survived in the index from 1959.

1959	2020
Allied Chemical Corporation	The Goldman Sachs Group, Inc.
Aluminum Company of America	American Express Company
American Can Company	Apple Inc.
American Telephone and Telegraph Company	The Boeing Company
American Tobacco Company (B shares)	Caterpillar Inc.
Anaconda Copper Mining Company	Chevron Corporation
Bethlehem Steel Corporation	Cisco Systems, Inc.
Chrysler Corporation	The Coca-Cola Company
E.I. du Pont de Nemours & Company	Dow Chemical Company
Eastman Kodak Company	Exxon Mobil Corporation
General Electric Company	Pfizer Inc.
General Foods Corporation	The Home Depot, Inc.
General Motors Corporation	Intel Corporation
Goodyear Tire and Rubber Company	International Business Machines Corporation
International Harvester Company	Johnson & Johnson
International Nickel Company, Ltd.	JPMorgan Chase & Co.
International Paper Company	McDonald's Corporation
Johns-Manville Corporation	Merck & Co., Inc.
Owens-Illinois, Inc.	Microsoft Corporation
The Procter & Gamble Company	Nike, Inc.
Sears Roebuck & Company	The Procter & Gamble Company
Standard Oil Co. of California	Raytheon Technologies
Standard Oil Co. of New Jersey	The Travelers Companies, Inc.
Swift & Company	UnitedHealth Group Inc.
Texaco Incorporated	Verizon Communications, Inc.
Union Carbide Corporation	Visa Inc.
United Aircraft Corporation	Walgreens Boots Alliance, Inc.
United States Steel Corporation	Walmart Inc.
Westinghouse Electric Corporation	The Walt Disney Company
F. W. Woolworth Company	3M Company

Figure 11. Comparison of Dow Jones Index, 1959-2020.

Perhaps if we look at a broader-based index, like the FTSE 100, we would see a different picture? Not really. The FTSE 100 index was started 36 years ago, in 1984, by the Financial Times newspaper and the Stock Exchange (hence FTSE), and includes the 100 largest companies by capitalisation traded on the London Stock Exchange. Even looking back only 36 years, there are only 19 companies that have remained on the index throughout.[29] Several have been removed and re-entered, but the list of 19 is given here. So even our very largest companies are not very good at staying at the top of the economy for long periods of time. That's not to say they have disappeared, or been taken over, or merged – although many have – but their position at the top of the financial hierarchy has changed substantially.

FTSE 100
British American Tobacco (BAT Industries)
Barclays
BP (British Petroleum)
GlaxoSmithKline (Glaxo Holdings)
Land Securities
Legal & General
Lloyds Banking Group (Lloyds bank)
Marks & Spencer
Pearson (Pearson (s) & Son)
Prudential (Prudential Corporation)
Reckitt Benckiser (Reckitt & Colman)
RELX Group (Reed International)
Rio Tinto
RBS Group (Royal Bank of Scotland)
Sainsbury's (J Sainsbury)
Royal Dutch Shell
Smith & Nephew
Tesco
Unilever

Figure 12. Companies in the FTSE 100 since its foundation.

The learning from these examples is that businesses have to reinvent themselves continuously. Those that are clever enough to take the radical decisions necessary have a better chance of survival. An example close to home for me is IBM. When I joined in 1981, it was a business dominated by hardware rental and sales. Its 1981 archive report tells us of the launch of many new hardware lines. Software and services are not mentioned at all.[30]

By the time I left in 2019, hardware represented less than 10% of revenues, and the key service lines (Business and Technology services) made up 57% of revenue. It's a great example of a company that knows it has to change at least as fast as the market does, although our earlier case study shows that the strategy has been questionable over significant periods. I think of the ability and willingness to change as being more part of the company's culture than its strategy – perhaps what has saved it over the years.

Why do I feel it's necessary to make this point? It's because many strategies I read are, when you get past all the surrounding verbiage, a plea to be left alone to do what the organisation is already doing.

There's another way to look at change, particularly relevant if you are being given targets and assets to shape and implement your strategy. In a medium to large organisation, a divisional, functional or area leader is often given a target to make (or a mission if, for example, you are part of a government owned/led organisation) together with a budget and headcount. In my experience, the targets usually go up each year, and the resources go down. So, if you are building a strategy, it needs to allow for this annual tightening of the options you have.

Another way to look at it is productivity. Let's take an example, where the targets go up by 3% each year, and the headcount goes down by 3% each year. Over a three year period:

Year 1: target is 100, headcount is 100. Productivity is 1 unit per person.

Year 2: target is 103, headcount is 97. Productivity is 1.06 units per person.

Year 3: target is 106.1, headcount is 94 (rounded down). Productivity is 1.13 units per person.

Over that three year period, your team has to become 13% more productive per head. And in a commercial organisation, this trend is likely to be ongoing. Don't expect it to stop. All too often, this leads to a 'salami slicing' approach to strategy, which simply says we'll ask everyone to work just that bit longer, and just that bit harder, and we'll cope. How many times have you (or your boss) said 'work smarter, not harder' when faced with these challenges?

Some of these productivity problems can be helped – or even solved for a while – by new technology. It does make a difference, but usually at a price in both capital and expense, and also in retraining and rewriting processes. But the strategy writer should be looking at the organisational culture and realising that the productivity improvements required are one of the key environmental changes that should be factored into the strategy so that the plan you write embraces the challenge by looking for big productivity drivers, such as

- New routes to market.

- New business models.

- Adopting new technology such as AI.

It should also spur you on to benchmark your productivity against your leading competitors and (much more interestingly) the very best peers or equivalent in any industry, learning from other industries how they approach what are often very similar problems. Other organisations who don't compete against you are also much more likely to be willing to share with you how they achieve their excellence than people in the same industry.

The difference between business as usual and strategy

One of the most frequent mistakes I see when strategies are presented is the failure to distinguish between business as usual (BAU) activities and strategy. This seems like an obvious thing to avoid, but a lot of papers contain this error. It is particularly true for functional parts of the organisation such as HR, IT or communications. It is often a symptom of a lack of overall strategic guidance from the top of the company. If your leaders do not require change and support for that change, it's easy to see how a functional strategy created in a vacuum could take a 'steady as she goes' approach to its own planning.

For example, a strategy paper from IT might contain a key action to implement the very latest and strongest security software and protocols. But what on earth is an IT department doing if it is not providing a secure environment? This is pure 'housekeeping'. There is no strategic advantage to be gained in a commercial or non-commercial environment from this. It's vitally important, of course, to protect customer, supplier, employee etc. data, and to prevent unauthorised access to your systems. Now that GDPR has been in place for several years, most boards are very much aware of the risks, and the penalties can be severe. All this means is that every single organisation in the EU (and any others that will be trading with the EU) must take appropriate steps to manage data, permissions etc. It's a *foundational* activity. What do I mean by a foundational activity?

It's any necessary activity that has to be performed by the organisation that doesn't distinguish it in any way or which adds no strategic value. For example, accounting for your finances is a mandatory activity, essential for any organisation, and is extremely unlikely to feature in your strategic thinking.

Let's say there are two levels of BAU activity (it doesn't matter whether there are more, the point remains the same); cross-company activity and functional activity. Cross-company activities would be common across all or most parts of the organisation. These would include administrative processes, HR processes and financial processes. Functional BAU activity would be the bread and butter actions of individual parts of the organisation. For example, the communications team would handle requests from the press for interviews; the IT function would provide laptops or mobile devices to employees; HR would ensure that people get paid on time each month. There are multiple activities that each function performs that it has to do, and which are taken for granted as the base level of work that they should perform.

On top of these activities are those that are more discretionary and those which add more value: these are the ones that become interesting from a strategic point of view. If we draw a simple picture to represent this for a hypothetical communications department:

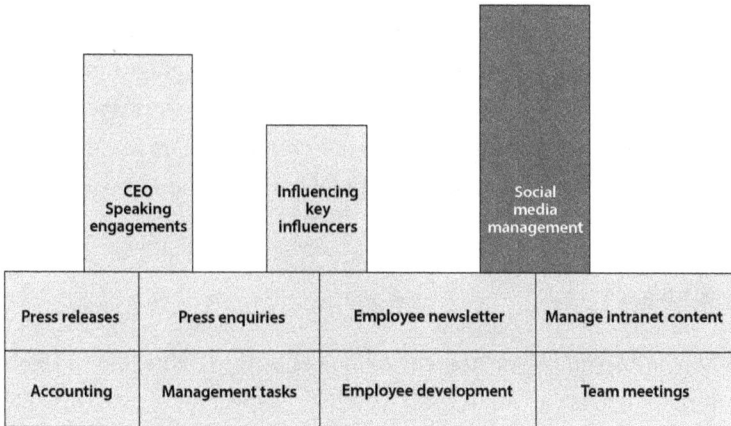

Figure 13. BAU and selected strategic activities.

As you can see in the diagram, there are three distinct layers of activity. The bottom layer would be very similar for any part of the organisation and has nothing unique to communications. The second layer represents what any communications department would have to do. There are few opportunities to gain strategic advantage from these tasks, although there is clearly an operational purpose in performing them, as well as a values and culture imperative to execute them with excellence, but those two layers are BAU.

On top of these, I have put three different examples of where the department might choose to focus its strategic intent. The different heights of the bars show that there will be different emphasis placed on different elements. In this example, managing social media takes the most effort, followed by managing the CEO's external speaking engagements and lastly, working on influencing the people identified as key influencers for your organisation and perhaps industry.

The key element here is that there is very little discretion about the two base layers. Any management attention focused here will be on effective performance and governance (especially for the company-wide layer) and on becoming more efficient at getting these things done. Any efficiencies here can immediately free up time to be spent on the strategic actions. Management focus and interest should be on the three key activities on the top layer. There can be fewer or more than three, of course. When we get to the next section on strategic actions, I will consider the numbers.

The lesson for anyone writing a strategy is not to see BAU activities as strategic.

There is also an important way to look at how to define the strategic intent, which is gap analysis. If you have a specific target to aim for, and you can see clearly that your existing (BAU) activities, even with optimistic productivity assumptions, will not meet the target, the question is, what else *could* you do to fill the gap? The figure here gives an example.

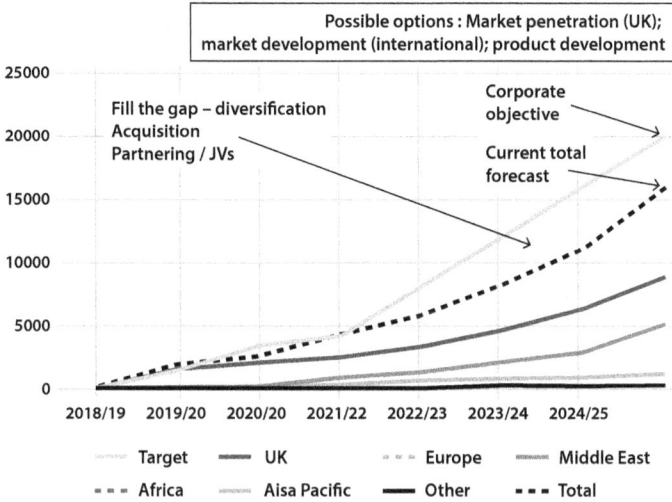

Figure 14. Gap analysis and possible responses.

The options shown are not a complete list, more a prompt to get the thinking started about how the gap can be closed in the long-term. Realising that there is a gap is the essential piece of work, and then the analysis can start to look at options to close it.

Deciding your strategic intent

"Strategy is about setting yourself apart from the competition. It's not a matter of being better at what you do — it's a matter of being different at what you do."

Michael Porter (Management guru and author)

Given that there are two origins for a strategy, situational or goal-driven, we can arrive at a strategic intent from two different directions. The quality of the intent, either way, depends on how good your analytical work has been.

The classical commercial model as defined by Michael Porter is that there are three generic strategy options:

1. Overall cost leadership.

2. Differentiation.

3. Focus.

This isn't a bad place to start. He points out that it is all but impossible to select more than one of these options: "Effectively implementing any one of these generic strategies usually requires total commitment and supporting organisational arrangements that are diluted if there is more than one target." Note also that a low-cost strategy is not the same as a low price one. Having low costs gives you the option to make more or less margin at different times and in different places without causing unmanageable problems around profitability.

"We will never try to develop a strategy that wins on price. There is nothing unique about pricing." This quotation is from Josh S Weston, former chair and CEO of Automatic Data Processing. A strategy based on competing on price is always going to lose unless you are the low-cost producer – in which case, your strategy is to be low cost.

However, this isn't necessarily helpful when applied to charities or especially government bodies. An NHS Trust doesn't have the choice to select options one, two and even, to a certain extent, three, for example.

The strategic intent outlines an overall approach for overcoming the obstacles you have identified during your analysis work. It is not a definition of what actions to take – that comes in the third section, where you define them. Richard Rumelt calls this approach drawing on your 'sources of advantage'. W Chan Kim and Renee Mauborgne talk about blue ocean strategies having three key characteristics: focus, divergence and a compelling tagline. By this, they mean that first of all, you have to choose what to focus on; you then need to create some clear differentiation between your organisation and its competition; and finally, you have to be able to summarise what your approach is in a clear, simple and brief way.

We can see some clear themes coming out of these different approaches to working out the 'what' of your strategy. I prefer to think about this as a way to decide about **focus** and **concentration**.

Focus is all about deciding your priorities. Concentration is then about applying your resources to your priorities.

Let's look at some examples of strategic intent, some simple, some more complex.

- Ikea Sustainability: "Together with co-workers, customers, and partners the world over, we are tackling climate change, unsustainable consumption, and inequality."[31]

- Unilever: "To be the global leader in sustainable business, showing that our purpose-led, future-fit business model delivers superior performance. We're guided in that by five strategic choices."[32]

- Tesla: "To achieve the transition to sustainable energy, we must produce more affordable EVs [Electric Vehicles] and energy storage, while building factories faster and with far less investment."[33]

- HSBC: "[Our strategy] includes targets for accelerating the shift of capital to areas, principally Asia and wealth, that have demonstrated the highest returns and where we have sustainable advantage through scale. Our international network remains a key competitive advantage, and we will continue to support cross-border banking flows between major trade corridors. Supported by these shifts, we are aiming to reach mid-single-digit revenue growth in the medium to long-term, with a higher proportion of our revenue from fee and insurance income."[34]

To illustrate this, I'd like to tell the story of a high-profile strategy that made a huge impact on the political landscape of the UK for over a decade and which has echoes today.

Case Study: The Labour party 1997 election campaign

I was lucky enough to be able to spend some time discussing this campaign with Alan Barnard. He was involved with developing the communications strategy for the Labour party's election win in 1997, which swept Tony Blair into power with a majority of 179, the largest it has ever had. Alan Barnard has spent his working life as a campaigner and played a key role in overhauling Labour's campaign methods during the 1990s, first at constituency level, then from 1993 at head office where he became the Labour party's director of campaigns and elections.

Alan had been campaigning for the Labour party for some time, both as a volunteer and then employed, and his local successes led to invitations to work on larger and larger campaigns. He was curious, inventive and entrepreneurial, always wanting to work out how to be more effective and more efficient at mobilising people to take action. Alan's local campaigns were often where new ideas were developed and tested, and he was always on the lookout for a new idea to incorporate into campaign communications.

One major opportunity to learn came when Alan (along with two colleagues) volunteered for the first Clinton-Gore campaign in the US that led to Clinton's election as president in 1992. He came back brimming with ideas for improving message discipline, rapid rebuttal and attack, and fundraising.

As Alan looked at the Labour party's disappointing results from the 1992 election, which had seen the rival Conservative party returned to power with a small majority, he had to make some key decisions based on everything he had learned in his previous campaigns and in the US. Alan had fought the 1992 election in a constituency campaign, so he had been on the receiving end of the campaign strategy as delivered by the head office of the time. He didn't think the targeting strategy used in 1992 had been clinical enough. Back then, it was delivered to specific demographics within the population (mostly those that could be easily identified) who were told information related to their demographic. So, nurses (who could be targeted if they lived in nurses' accommodation) were told how bad things were in the NHS, instead of being told things that were less obvious and might get them to change their vote (such as how Labour could be trusted on the economy).

Alan had been developing a database to target voters based on their previous voting intentions and behaviours. He knew how many votes cast for Labour on polling day were needed to win, and he knew how many people would (probably always) vote Labour and who would never do so (and where they lived). But there were never enough Labour voters, so he had to put together a coalition of voters for each election to reach his target number of votes, made up of people who might change their voting allegiances from election to election. Alan targeted his communications based on previous and potential future voting behaviour. Importantly, they would all get broadly the same information and messaging based on the overarching story aimed at voters in general. The previous approach had been to aim specific messages at particular demographics in what might be thought of as a 'retail offering'. This would be his first big change when he moved to Labour's head office.

So, Alan ripped up the campaign strategy that had been used in the past. He realised that even getting a fantastic turn-out by Labour voters would not be enough to win. His analysis showed they had to concentrate on Conservative voters who potentially would switch to Labour. Specifically, the team identified 92 constituencies that would move to Labour with a swing of six per cent or less. As Alan puts it: "We knew we had to reach out to voters we called 'switchers' because the electoral mathematics showed there were just not enough natural Labour supporters for us to win. This was a mistake that Labour had made time after time, thinking that if we only could explain our 'Labour-ness' better, voters would see the light and come flooding to us."

But how to go about this? They needed to make some fundamental changes to the ways the local Labour party members and activists, who were all volunteers, went about their campaigning. Everyone was an 'expert' campaigner, and they all had strong views about the right way to run a campaign – frequently at odds with the selected strategy.

The approach adopted was to increase hugely the numbers of professional organisers who would be working in each of the 92 targeted constituencies and invest in them to lead the culture change on a day-to-day basis. This was the strategic intent for their strategy. The three key volunteers in each seat had regular dialogue and training alongside the professional organisers, both at a regional and a national level.

Labour ended up with three target groups of voters based on voting history: 'switchers' from Tory, Lib Dem or nationalist; Lib Dem voters whose second preference would be Labour (i.e. anti-Tory voters, so-called 'squeeze' voters); Labour supporters whose voting history demonstrated they did not vote at every election ('weak Labour') and who needed both motivation and practical organisational help to vote. A forensic approach to data analysis gave the detail that was necessary, based on voting in all forms of elections (national, local, European, mayoral etc.). The voting records, of course, do not show which party someone voted for, but they do show who voted (strictly speaking, who was issued a ballot paper). Matching these with stated voting intentions revealed by canvassing gave sufficient information to determine who to target.

They retained just one target group based on demographics: all those who had turned 18 since the last election in April 1992, the 'first-time' voters. Research showed that if all of this demographic voted, they would support Labour in huge numbers, so it became more efficient to target them all rather than eliminate just a small subset from each communication. But, apart from practical information about how to vote, these voters would only receive the same messaging as everyone else from Labour rather than anything deemed to be specifically of interest to this age range.

Huge effort went into explaining to party activists why the approach was being adopted and then how to execute it. All performance targets and indicators were designed to measure progress towards segmenting the electorate into those target groups in each of the 92 seats, and then to deliver high-quality communications, repeatedly, that were designed to build their desire to vote Labour and to support, reassure and reinforce that they had taken the right decision.

Support from the regions and head office was professional and timely; communications materials such as leaflets and letters were of a higher quality than had been seen before, in terms of production quality, presentation and content. And there was more of it. Money was being spent better, and perceptions of success and professionalism on the road to a victory created more success and more fundraising, which led to a virtuous and self-sustaining cycle.

The result of all this is, of course, a matter of history. The Labour government was swept to power on a wave of hope and enthusiasm, with a record majority. Perhaps, as Alan concedes, they could have won without his local campaigns because the national messaging was so good. But the campaign was part of a set of communications that persuaded the nation that not only were Labour electable; they were simply a better choice than the Conservatives. With elections, there is no controlled experiment. There's no chance to do an A-B test on a vote. The result is what counts, and they over-delivered.

Learnings:

We can see very clear analysis to understand in detail what the electoral mathematics were and what the implications were. The strategic analysis delivered an uncomfortable message: that the previous strategy had been completely wrong. It's often hard for an organisation to accept that it has been mistaken and needs to adopt a different approach. In this case, the new leadership of the party provided the background that allowed this to be taken on board.

The strategic analysis was notable for being highly specific. The answer was to target precisely 92 seats, and for every single seat, the team knew *exactly* how many votes were needed to convert that seat to Labour. They knew that they needed to target 3 voters in order to win 2 votes – this came from the detailed analysis in previous successful local campaigns, as Alan had made a point of keeping records year after year.

The simple strategic intent was: 'we will target 92 seats that we can win with a swing of 6% or less'. That's a great example of what a strategic intent should look like. They had the 'why' provided by the strategic analysis. This was the 'what'. Note that the intent isn't about the actions that will follow. It's short, simple and could even be called a 'compelling tagline'.

Like all good strategies, it involves a clear choice. It tells the organisation what it is going to do, and by implication, what it is not going to do. It selects the one thing that it is going to do really well. It's not that there would be no activity in secure Labour seats or in the harder to win Conservative seats; obviously, there would be. But the management focus would be on one and only one thing: the 92 seats.

Following on from that, the 'how' was delivered by the small number of key actions of educating the volunteers and activists in the 92 seats and making sure that everyone, from top to bottom, knew the five pledges and stayed on message.

Lastly, the communication of the strategy (internal) and the strategy of communication (external) were consistent, reinforced time and time again by each communications channel. Five straightforward value-based messages that had been put together based on the real intent (and hence 'authentic' – a word I dislike, but which is appropriate in this case) took the story that the campaign wanted to tell and made it real through examples.

It's (literally) a textbook example of a strategy.

Our next example is Lexus, who entered the luxury car market in the late 1980s. Back in 1989, when the first model was launched, it quickly achieved success – but what lay behind that success? The market for prestige cars at the time was dominated by a handful of manufacturers: Rolls Royce and Bentley at the top, but with tiny volumes. Mercedes dominated the market, with some BMW models competing; Jaguar – at the time – had a reputation for poor quality and in 1990 was bought by Ford before being sold to Tata Motors in 2008.

Toyota had found out that their brand would not permit them to enter this market under their own badge, so they had to create an entirely new brand. Their strategic intent was: "Better than Mercedes quality for a mid-premium price." To achieve this took a huge investment, and a remarkable focus on a small number of strategic actions: emphasis on a superior product (not just matching the Mercedes offering); a winning value proposition; superior customer service; winning over the industry influencers, such as JD Power.

Note that their advertising slogan: 'The relentless pursuit of perfection', is not the same as their strategic intent.

We all know the result: the LS400 reset the benchmark for quality and value and sold extremely well. Since then, Lexus remains a significant player in the quality car market, but competition has meant that the gap between them and others is much closer, and the differential is much less marked.

How to word the strategic intent

If your strategic intent is going to be of any use, it must state clearly what direction you are going to take. It doesn't have to explain why; that is needed when getting approval or when communicating the strategy. It should link back to your organisational purpose and vision and clearly take you in a direction that is consistent with both statements. It's an important test of the intent that it should reinforce rather than contradict (or be disconnected from) your purpose and vision.

A common pitfall when writing the intent is to re-hash the purpose or vision. These underpin the strategy; they are not the same thing. The purpose informs the strategy, and the vision should be demonstrably nearer if the strategy is successful.

Logically, because the strategic intent sits between the strategic analysis and strategic actions, it bridges between the two. If the strategic analysis is the 'why', then the strategic intent is the 'what', and the strategic actions are the 'how'. So if you were to write a short summary of the strategy you might structure it like this:

"There are several factors that we need to take into account as we perform our planning. These are factors a, b, c and d. [Strategic analysis]

In order to address them, we need to direct ourselves in a specific way, with focus on x and y. [Strategic intent]

Therefore we will take the following initiatives over the period of the plan: 1, 2, 3, 4 and 5. [Strategic actions]"

When publishing the strategic intent, you may well omit the sections on strategic analysis and strategic actions or keep them separate for more detailed communications.

Of course this is greatly oversimplified, but the structure may help you to write down the intent.

If you started out with one or more goals to make (goal-based strategy), then the intent needs to be clear what you are going to do to make those goals. Let's look at an example. If your goal is to increase revenue by 15% over the next three years (this is not necessarily a good goal, as we have seen), then your strategic intent may be:

"We will expand into Germany and France by building a sales and distribution capability in those two countries" or perhaps, "We will introduce a product range to meet the emerging new segment of buyers that we have identified" or perhaps, "We will accept lower margins over the next three years to allow us to invest in more marketing and an increased sales force."

For a non-commercial organisation, such as a government department, the goal would be different, and the strategic intent would also have a different dimension – perhaps about how the budget is to be used or about hiring policies to bring on the required new talent.

If, on the other hand, you are designing a situation-based strategy, your strategic intent will be about how you will address the situation:

"We will create a new division to achieve first entry into this new market", or "We will divert non-essential resources into one division to allow us to focus on this emerging problem."

There has to be enough substance to the intent to derive real and substantial actions from it. To make a very simple analogy, it's like saying: "For our holiday, we will travel to Scotland." The direction is clear, but you decide later whether to fly, drive or go by train.

Avoid the use of easy – but meaningless – clichés, such as: "We will become a world-class, agile organisation", or "We will provide best-of-breed products to the market", neither of which give any indication of what actions should be taken. These are neither strategic intent nor strategic actions; they're just examples of business buzzwords that are over-used.

There are no hard and fast rules about how long a strategic intent should be. If you have got beyond two or three sentences, you have probably got too much, are losing clarity or haven't done the necessary thinking to reach a concise answer.

What happens if you are not sure where to start? This is not an unusual situation. Even with an excellent piece of work on strategic analysis, it may be that you see too many possible options and that none is leaping out at you as 'the answer'.

Martin Thomas, author of *Social Media Strategy*, is a fan of what he calls 'laddering up'. He means start with something that you know works. It may be small; it may be unnoticed; it may be obvious or not. However, if you have some element of what you do already that you know works with your customers, and is stealing a march on the competition, you may have the basis for a broader idea. Don't discard it just because you didn't find it through analysis. You can perform the analysis now to see why it works and whether it has broader applicability.

What is the relationship between goals and a strategic intent?

If you have one or more goals to achieve, and this is why you are creating a strategy, this is an easy question to answer. Your strategic intent lays out what you will do to meet those goals. If, on the other hand, your strategy is situational, then you don't have to have decided your goal(s) when laying out the strategic intent (see Figure 3, *The relationship between strategy types and goals*). However, no strategy is complete without goals, and you must ask yourself the question about how you will know whether your strategy has succeeded. This will mean you need to know two things:

1. What will you measure to determine success?

2. What threshold must you attain, by when, to confirm that you have done what you decided to do?

Goals have been extensively discussed previously. You can decide on one overarching target for your strategy, or you can define several goals in the next part of the process – defining strategic actions.

Strategic intent and focus

This is the stage in the process of creating a strategy where you have to make real decisions about how to deploy the resources of your organisation. These choices involve selection from the many different possibilities that could provide the same outcome. They involve de-selection as well. There is no organisation that can select every option and then discard all the less effective ones after a while. Even if you had the time and resources to do that, it would be organisationally impossible to rally round multiple options to achieve the same goals. So you have to focus. That means making clear choices – effectively you are placing a bet on the best way to achieve what you are trying to do. Like all betting, you can improve the odds by understanding as much as you can about the situation: that's what the strategic analysis process is for. If you did a good job there, you will have insights into the various paths open to you and will be able to relate these to organisational capabilities.

This part of strategy creation is another area of common failings that I see. It's tough to make a firm choice. It's even tougher to decide to stop doing something. But let's look at the logic. If you have to achieve change – significant change – then you can't just continue as you are. So, pick a strategic direction and be bold enough to realise that this means that you expend less effort and resource somewhere else. If you are going to apply additional resources in support of your direction, they have to come from somewhere; in most cases, this means diverting people and money from existing activities so that you can invest in the chosen area.

If you leave all your resources exactly where they are, then it's very unlikely you will be able to drive the level of change needed. Even if the only thing that you change is the amount of time you personally spend on the chosen priority, that's a big signal to the organisation of what you care about. And we all know (in the words of one of my bosses) 'what interests my manager fascinates me'. Spending more time with one division, for example, means spending less elsewhere.

In the 1990s, Lou Gerstner made a clear decision: IBM would become an integrator of technology rather than just a provider. A huge change, that needed big investments – for example, the purchase of the consulting business of PWC in 2002, the same year Gerstner handed over the reins of IBM to his successor. Making integration the focus meant a (big) move away from being primarily a hardware company. Toyota made the decision to launch an entirely new brand: Lexus. This was a big, risky bet. And it worked because their strategic intent had focus. They invested in creating a whole new company, brand and set of products. Alan Barnard's strategy was to rip up the way the Labour party had campaigned and focus their resources on 92 winnable seats – and at the same time diverting effort and resources away from the firm Labour seats.

Conclusions:

A strategic intent should have change at its heart; your rate of change has to keep up with the external world but not run so far ahead that you lose the connection with those you serve. Don't make business as usual your strategy. No organisation can do everything, so don't let your strategy fudge issues in an attempt to keep everyone happy. Your strategic intent must have focus: this is where you place your big bets. Make choices. Take risks. Be very clear about what you are not doing, just as much as what you are. Make your strategic intent clear and brief.

Tests for your strategy:

1. Can you summarise your strategic intent clearly, simply and briefly?

2. Does your strategic intent take you towards your vision if successfully executed?

3. Does your strategic intent require the organisation to change at least as fast as the eternal environment?

4. Does your strategic intent lay out the priorities?

5. Is it clear from your strategic intent what you are not going to focus on?

6. Does your strategic intent play to your strengths?

CHAPTER 6

The Essence of a Strategy: Strategic Actions

"Dreams only come true when you appoint strategic consistent actions to wake you up."

Edmond Mbiaka (Thinker and guru)

Now we have our 'general direction', but there is nothing to tell us how we are going to implement this strategic intent. So we need some actions. These are not just the kinds of actions that we take in the minutes of a meeting: operational or tactical actions. These are the key things we need to do if our strategic intent is to achieve what we need it to.

A strategy needs to have three characteristics if it is to succeed.

1. It must be the *right (or best) thing* to do.

2. It must be *executable.*

3. It must be *executed.*

The previous two sections, if done properly, will have reassured you that you have selected the right thing to do. This section looks at the second part, creating actions that are executable.

The third characteristic, which is about the translation of your strategy from paper to reality, is discussed in Chapter 7.

Before we set about looking at whether the strategic actions are executable, I'll explain what I mean by a strategic action, as opposed to any other kind of action.

A strategic action will:

1. Address one or more of the strategy's objectives in a substantive way.

2. Have a timeline for execution that complements the strategy's.

3. Allow operational flexibility in its implementation.

4. Be consistent with the other strategic actions.

The first of these means that your action should – if executed – meet a significant part of the strategic intent. An action may address more than one of the strategy's goals. For example, you may set a strategy that is to invest significantly more in research and development. This could address a strategic objective to move faster than the competition in addressing a new market. It could also contribute to a strategy to hire the best people in the market. It should not be a small action that only covers a part of the intent. That comes later when looking at how to operationalise the strategy.

The second characteristic will ensure that the strategic action remains valid during the lifetime of the strategy – or most of it. An action that only applies in year one is, by definition, an operational action, not a strategic one. If there's an action that sits uncomfortably between operational and strategic but is nonetheless essential, don't get hung up on the labels, but ensure it is captured and will be executed.

The third characteristic, operational flexibility, is essential because while it should provide direction, it should not tie the hands of the leadership team in such a way that it does not allow for the inevitable problems and changes that will come. In a simplistic example, if the strategy is to hire the best talent in the industry, then the operational plan, covering 12 months, might have a list of the preferred people to hire, but the strategic plan would not. The strategic action would remain flexible because it would allow for individuals to retire, become ill, move country, change career or refuse to work for you under any circumstances.

Lastly, consistency. Clearly the strategic actions should be consistent with each other, but this may not always be as easy as it sounds. Consider a strategy that says a company will focus heavily on digital marketing and sales. It may also state that high-value sales will continue to be sold by a channel of business partners. Sounds consistent – but is it? The business partners will almost certainly watch your digital strategy unfold and interpret it – correctly or incorrectly – as a direction that will gradually, but inevitably, reduce reliance on them as a route to market for the higher priced products. So they may quietly open discussions with your competitors as their safety net should their fears come to pass – and suddenly, you may find high-value sales being lost to competitors while your digital channel is struggling to bring in large volumes of lower value sales.

Another example might be a strategy that has actions to become the most efficient player in your market while at the same time attracting the best talent to work for you. 'Most efficient' is almost always translated as 'lowest cost', while attracting the best talent means you will have to pay very attractive salaries and provide great working conditions. These may be two actions that cause a lot of internal struggle because they really are not consistent with each other.

Consistency is also important for large organisations when looking across functions, divisions and areas. If your Asia Pacific region decides that it will prioritise one division's products because of the favourable market conditions for that product set, there may be considerable upset for the other divisions, who expect the amount of investment and management time in Asia Pacific that they receive in other regions.

If you have written down more than a handful of strategic actions (probably between three and seven), then stop. Having more than that number means you will not have the right focus, and you are not making the tough choices. One organisation I worked with had a draft strategy with dozens of actions, which would have been impossible to prioritise, communicate and allow effective board supervision. They ended up with five, making the difficult decisions about what they would, and would not, do.

Let's take a look at a case study that shows the value of understanding the right strategic actions.

Case Study: Gramophone magazine

Gramophone is an iconic classical music magazine published in the UK. It was founded in 1923 by the Scottish author and playwright Compton MacKenzie, best known for *Whisky Galore* and *The Monarch Of The Glen*, both of which have been turned into films and TV series. After a while, he tired of the enterprise and sold the rights to the Pollard family, who owned the title until 1999, when it was acquired by Haymarket.

I found this out from Mark Allen, chairman of the Mark Allen Group (MAG), who are the current owners of *Gramophone*. He explained that he had been setting up a meeting with Haymarket's broker over the phone and casually enquired whether they had any titles for sale. "Yes," was the answer, "but you wouldn't be interested." The Agent's logic was that music magazines were not (then) part of the MAG publishing activities. As it turned out, Mark was interested, and although there was already a potential buyer lined up, he met the tight deadline of just one week to put together and confirm a bid. The growing reputation of the group was the clincher for the deal, and *Gramophone* moved across to join what is now a stable of more than 100 titles.

Mark told me the fascinating story of how they completely changed the strategy for the magazine and turned around its fortunes.

When *Gramophone* was founded, it was as a reviews magazine for classical music. It was very successful in this niche for decades, building a name for itself as the top place to find classical music reviews. However, when Haymarket took it over, they decided to reposition it as having broader coverage of the whole classical music scene. This brought it into head-to-head competition with BBC Music Magazine, launched in 1992, which not only had the marketing might of the BBC behind it but was also linked to BBC Radio 3. Not surprisingly, *Gramophone* struggled and was losing its way – hence Haymarket's willingness to sell.

It had a subscription fee of £40 per annum and, even then, was finding things hard. It was a low price for what was primarily an affluent, middle-class readership, but the pricing of the rival magazine prevented them from increasing the subscription.

Mark told me of the goal-oriented strategy that the new owners put in place. The goals were simple: stop the slide into irrelevance, build on the strong brand, increase subscriptions and increase profitability.

It was clear that *Gramophone* had lost any distinctiveness in its market position. How could this be improved? Mark went back to the heritage of the long-running title: it started life as a reviews magazine and had been very successful for decades before Haymarket moved it to more general classical music coverage.

MAG took the following strategic actions:

1. They expanded and improved the editorial content of the brand.

They placed the key emphasis on the reviews section of the magazine, which was developed and repositioned. By doing so, they introduced clear water between themselves and BBC Music Magazine. It was essential to bring the management team with them on this, so a lot of time and effort was spent to get the marketing manager (who had to promote the newly positioned magazine and was at first highly sceptical about such bold steps but became a keen advocate) and the editor (who had to make sure it had all the right content) on board for this major change of direction.

The reviews section of the magazine was expanded and moved towards the front; they gave their reviewers greater licence and introduced some new ones; they emphasised that the reviews were totally independent (there was a suspicion, at the time, that the reviews were dependent on advertising); and they changed from a somewhat formulaic recipe to a much more fluid one. Haymarket had a standard for reviews of 200 words, no matter what the review was about.

Mark put it simply: "If a piece of music merited a paragraph, that's all it should get. On the other hand, we could put more emphasis on important reviews and give them the space they deserved."

2. Improved printing quality.

By using better quality paper for the front page in particular, they were able to improve the print reader's experience. Interestingly, because of the deals that they had been able to strike with printers and paper suppliers, this didn't result in increased costs. The magazine also expanded in size – again without increasing paper and print costs.

3. Increase subscription rates.

By being bold and stepping out from the shadow of direct competition with BBC Music, they were able to increase the subscription rates from, at the time, £40 to £60. They introduced three separate and identical platforms to which people could subscribe, each for the same £60 price point: print, digital or, thirdly, a database of reviews accumulated over many years. In practice, they were able to raise the price and also expand the readership.

4. Create a loyalty programme.

In addition, they also introduced Gramophone Club membership. If you wanted all three platforms – print, digital and the reviews database – you could get all three by subscribing for (at the time) £99. This brought a very good response to the platform, which greatly helped to increase subscription yields.

5. Create a single mission for the magazine.

Mark quickly noticed that the editorial and sales teams had different understandings of *Gramophone's* raison d'etre. He solved the problem simply: he got the team to write and agree a mission statement for the magazine together, which is printed inside the front cover. It had to be simple and short, and the importance was not what it said to the readers but the fact that they had to create it jointly, and therefore agree on the mission.

6. Reduce costs.

The brand was over-staffed. Despite expanding the coverage, they reduced staffing and encouraged them to work in a slightly different way without, in any way, compromising on editorial quality. Far from impacting morale, the new focus on making the magazine successful has transformed the morale of the team, who know they are working on a premier title. This was helped by a hugely productive 'away day' with presentations in the morning to update them and then breaking into problem-solving groups, getting buy-in at every stage.

The result? *Gramophone* is now twice as profitable as it was during the final years under Haymarket. The morale of the staff working on the publication is higher than it has ever been. In 2018 subscription numbers increased, as well as yield, bucking the overall market trend for falling subscriptions.

Learnings:

What struck me from my conversation with Mark was that the group as a whole knows what it is doing. On the group website, I find: "Connecting specialist audiences with critical information," followed by "We inform. We educate. We inspire. We engage. We know our markets. We enable your business." These are not given titles, such as purpose or mission, but they feel to me like such. It's clear that this is a business that knows what it is about and plays to its strengths. Its strategy is built on solid foundations.

A second reason for the success of the strategy for *Gramophone* magazine was the clear understanding of the following – a good example of a thorough strategic analysis:

- The readership and potential readership.
- The key competitor – positioning, pricing, strengths and weaknesses.
- The history and essence of the Gramophone brand.
- The difference between value and costs.

As well as the recurring theme of providing clarity to the whole team on the strategy, getting buy-in and a unitary, focused execution.

However, the reason the case study is in this chapter is that the strategic actions were very clear, well laid out and effectively executed. In this case, having so many titles in the stable has allowed Mark to gain great experience and expertise in what works (and what doesn't), and so his formula for effective strategic action has led to the renewed success of a well-known magazine.

Writing the strategic actions

First of all, don't have too many. Things are complex enough in any organisation without having to balance too many strategic actions. The more you have, the harder it will be to keep them in line with the four criteria. Typically three-five is about right, but two could be appropriate for your company, and possibly six, but at that number, I would pay close attention to whether it was really necessary to have that many.

Your actions should be clear and brief. This is how the strategy execution will be explained. You already have the strategic intent; now you are laying out how the organisation will behave in response to that strategic intent.

Next, your strategic actions must be capable of being measured and must have clear targets and timescales. All too often, we see a strategic action like 'Be the best employer', which is so vague that it is almost useless. The best employer in the world? In your industry? In your local area? What does 'best' mean? Highest retention rate? Highest wages? Best employee engagement results? If you want to have a meaningful strategic goal, perhaps something like: 'Improve workforce satisfaction by reducing employee attrition rate to 5% and increasing employee engagement to 75% by 2025'.

Using the learning from Chapter 3, where goals were discussed, make sure that there is no ambiguity in what the target means or how it is to be measured.

Whether your strategy is situational or goal-based, you must make the goals clear at this point. Goals have been extensively discussed previously – this is where the goals and the strategy join together. Let's look at an example of how you could lay out a strategic action using the example we just discussed.

Strategic action	Measurement	Goal	1 year milestones
Improve workforce satisfaction	1. Attrition rate 2. Employee engagement as measured by average of four key questions.	1. less than 5% by 2025 year end 2. 75% or higher by 2025 year end	1. Reduce from current 11% to 9.5% or better 2. Improve from current 49% to 55% or better

Table 1. Layout for a strategic action.

I'm not suggesting this is the best strategic goal – but it's clear, brief, has SMART goals, and shows the short-term requirement to get on track. Are all your strategic goals laid out as clearly?

Strategic levers

When deciding on your strategy to achieve the objectives, you have three levers that you can press to implement your choices.

- Time.

- Money.

- People (which, of course, includes not just people, but also IT, buildings etc.).

To get your strategy underway, you will almost certainly need a mix of these three levers. In my experience, you never start with enough of these. Sometimes it's just one thing, perhaps time, that is the problem. In a difficult case, you may be short of all three. Some people have suggested to me that there are other levers, such as quality, that also apply. If that is a helpful way to look at things, by all means, use it. I prefer to think that the necessary quality is defined, explicitly or implicitly, in the objectives, and if quality can be compromised, then the objectives are not clear enough.

The one constant is the goal or set of goals that have to be met.

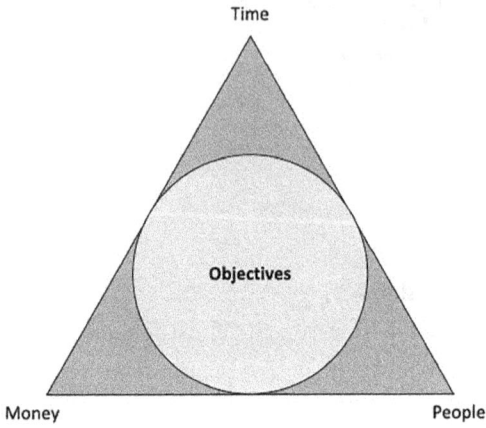

Figure 16. The resource triangle, where objectives and resources are matched.

If time is short, then the triangle presses down from the top, and it may be that more money or resource is needed. Similarly, if money is short, perhaps the timeline has some flexibility in it. The usual position is that people will feel that they are short of all three and that the objectives are not achievable. How you communicate the strategy will have a huge bearing on how your employees perceive the nature of the challenge, and the more they have been consulted and informed throughout the process, the more likely they are to help you find a path that leads to success, despite what seem like impossible hurdles at the start of the journey.

What happens if you don't have enough resources to make the target at all, despite all the inventiveness and productivity improvements that you can possibly summon? In short, the picture looks like this:

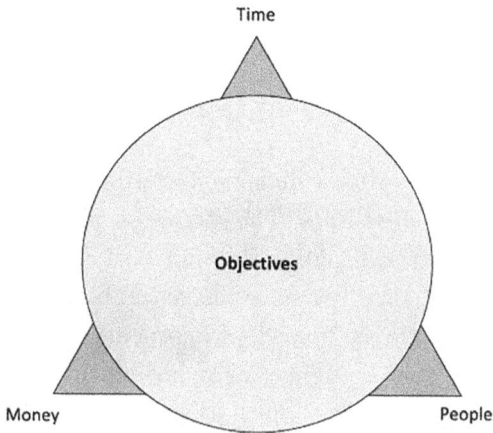

Figure 17. The resource triangle, where objectives and resources are not matched.

In this case, you have to make a choice. Will you change the objectives or change the resources? The former may not be possible if you are in a large organisation and are simply given the goals. The latter may also be difficult, if not impossible. In either case, a tough conversation needs to take place so that everyone can agree that resources match the targets.

Your analysis should tell you what the industry benchmarks are for these things. If your competitor (or sister organisation) has achieved something in two years, it's hard to argue that you can't do it in the same time, all other things being equal. If your competitor has a better E:R (expense to revenue) ratio for their sales force, you should be able to match it or understand what you need to do so. Only if your benchmarks tell you that no one has achieved the performance required of you does it make sense to fight hard to change the targets. Note, again, the value of time spent on good strategic analysis. The only other option is to rethink, radically, how you could meet the objectives with the resources you have.

Coming back to the point about the strategy being executable, you must be close, or close enough, to the three levers having a chance of success. To starve your implementation of one of these three things is setting yourself up for failure.

Here's where we get to a defining characteristic of strategies: where you **place your bets**. The success of any strategy worthy of the name will involve making decisions – often tough ones with significant consequences for those affected – about where to invest resources. There may be financial investments, but each element of the triangle is to be thought of as an investment. You place your people and use their time as much as you use capital or expense, and in this exercise, you use them in a way that supports your plan and maximises the value that they can all contribute.

Consider a strategy that prioritises attacking a new market. If you don't put in sufficient marketing and sales resources, you will fail. If you don't invest in the right products (or packaging, branding etc.) for that new market, you will fail. If you don't invest in new routes to market, the chances are you will fail. So far, so good. If you accept that these decisions mean the application of resources, that's the easy bit. The tough decision is where you take them from. This is the bit that people so often shy away from. Where do you *disinvest* to fund the necessary resources?

Again, I have seen a lot of strategies that depend on the 'magic money tree' to pay for the necessary people, infrastructure and operating budgets, with no consideration of how this can be provided. Strategy is as much about what you will stop doing as it is about where you will invest.

One of the best strategic conversations I had was with a boss who knew that he wanted to invest in digital marketing over the next three years. He defined what the goals would be for those three years (a 250% increase in revenue by the end of that period). We then sat down and went through the budgets, starting with the investments needed to support his strategy. Headcount was reduced elsewhere to provide the right skills to the digital marketing team; events budgets were cut; local marketing budgets were reduced so that there was a realistic amount of expense that allowed the digital programme to succeed. We balanced the overall budget and met milestones on the way to the ambitious target. Bets were placed – and were successful. You can't fudge your way to a working strategy. Bets placed on every outcome aren't bets.

This stage, therefore, is one that requires – probably – the most internal persuasion. Leaders who are quite happy to accept the strategic analysis and strategic intent are now faced with the reality of needing to see their budgets reduced to fund the necessary investments. Perhaps their pet projects are put on the back burner or cancelled because you are recommending that these should not be a priority. It's a purely human reaction to want to preserve the assets one has, and leaders are not exempt from this emotional response. It is unlikely that the money and people to be invested in the strategic actions will be entirely new; the chances are that some or all of it will come from existing budgets and headcount. This will be part of the political management of your strategy.

Once you have written down your actions, is that it? Do you have a strategy? Not quite. You're well down the road. But those actions, no matter how well-drafted, are subject to reality when you try to implement them. Spell out, therefore, as part of your strategy, what your risks, assumptions and dependencies are. By articulating these clearly at this stage, you may avoid problems during the execution of the strategy.

Conclusions:

Strategic actions take the strategic intent and turn it into the headings of the key things you will do to make it real. There will be a small number of strategic actions with SMART goals, definitions of what is to be measured and possibly some milestones for the period of the strategy. Matching the three key levers of time, money and resources will tell you about whether your investments are going to be sufficient to meet the objectives. You will also lay out the risks and dependencies of the strategy in this section.

Tests for your strategy:

1. Have you written a small number of clear strategic actions that support your strategic intent?

2. Has each action got a clear and measurable outcome?

3. Are the investments of time, money and resources sufficient to deliver the goals?

4. Are the investments going to be supported by the stakeholders?

5. Have you looked carefully at the risks, assumptions and dependencies and documented them?

6. Have you been clear about where you are focusing and where you are reducing focus/investment?

CHAPTER 7

Getting Your Strategy on Paper

"One day, I will find the right words, and they will be simple."

Kerouac (Novelist)

I'm going to assume that your strategy will be written down. This may be a big assumption because there are plenty of small organisations that have never written down their strategy. This doesn't mean that they don't have one – at least, it doesn't mean that they can't have one. It may be that with a small enough number of people, you can all agree – implicitly or explicitly – on what the strategy is. As ever, the quality of the thinking is the essence. Having said that, not writing it down is going to cause problems sooner or later: what happens when the chief exec leaves, or is on holiday? What happens when the organisation hits an unexpected roadblock? What happens when it emerges that different people have differing views of what the strategy actually is? What happens when you need to borrow money from the bank, and they want to see your strategy?

So, your strategy will be written down. How does that work in practice?

Who should write the strategy?

"The word processor is a better tool than a quill pen because you can do so much more with it, but on the other hand, what you have to say and how you say it is the ultimate determination."

Walter Murch (Film editor, writer, sound designer and Academy Award winner)

The chief executive is accountable for having an up-to-date and appropriate company strategy, but s(he) will not usually do the writing, although I would expect that s(he) will have a lot of input to the content and would certainly be a key person to sign off the draft. So who should hold the pen? I am guessing that the answer is you, dear reader.

One of my contacts who provided a case study for this book told me about a former manager who used to work in the strategy department of a UK quango (quasi-autonomous non-governmental organisation). He asked his boss: "What is the role of our department?" The response was 'to do what those above us are supposed to do, but for half of the salary'.

As the task involves gathering a lot of information, collating it, making sense of it, and working out the organisation response and changes needed, it will typically be someone within the organisation with a broad cross-functional view and enough experience to know what is important and what can be ignored. That's you.

If the organisation is big enough, then it's probably going to be a team putting it together. Whether it's you on your own or a large team, it is really important to get as many views as you can from all relevant sources.

If you have the luxury of putting a team together to do this, try to bring one or more people from different functions into the team writing the strategy, even if they don't see the whole picture (e.g. sensitive financials). You could even bring in customers, suppliers or business partners to specific parts of the process, not just as focus groups for testing ideas but for helping to formulate parts of the strategy itself – being careful about setting expectations and maintaining the right levels of confidentiality.

Whatever purpose the team fulfils, pull together people that bring real diversity to the exercise. If everyone thinks alike, you'll just end up with the same old thing you have always done. Bring in people from different backgrounds, ages, cultures...

Length

"Brevity is the soul of wit."

William Shakespeare

Strategies are often presented over hundreds of pages. I've seen one recently (Nov 2019) that was over 170 pages of dense text, tables and images. This isn't helpful when trying to get approvals and in communication. If it is very lengthy, then

- No one is going to read the whole document.

- Stakeholders will be concerned that the strategy is not clear or communicable.

- They may get the impression that there is no high-level view, which is worrying.

- They may think the strategy is trying to cover every eventuality.

- They may feel that the strategy cannot be understood and therefore executed.

All too often, the strategy paper becomes over-long because the operational plans for its execution are included in the strategy paper. The paper then tries to tell every audience everything that can possibly be told about the strategy and its execution.

Consider a strategy paper as the basis on which a situation is addressed or for meeting long-term goals. That's all. From the strategy, you should derive operational plans, which should be documented separately.

I think of a strategy paper as having three layers:

1. Executive summary.

2. Executive explanation.

3. Backup information.

There should be a *one page* Executive Summary for every strategy. If the strategy cannot be summarised on one page, **it is not ready for review**. How to present it is discussed in the section on getting approval for your strategy.

The next section should explain the strategy in more detail, at a level appropriate for the approver(s); this should be fairly brief. If you can't explain the strategy in fewer than 25 (easily readable)

PowerPoint pages or 5-8 (ditto) Word pages, it is probably too detailed.

Lastly, include an appendix that gives the details which are referred to in the strategy. This allows a reviewer to see the complete facts, data or other details that underpin the strategy without having to include them in the main body of the document. The appendix is the summary of the sources of information you have used to lay out the current situation, the explanation of your thinking where needed, and enough detail about the proposals you have made that a well-informed reader does not need to speak to you in person to understand how you reached your conclusion. A well-informed reader is someone who is familiar with your organisation: any of the executive team should be able to understand all the elements of the strategy based on these three layers. A non-executive director should also be able to grasp what you have laid out.

Style

"The book you read and read well, over and over again, lives in you, becomes your thought and thinking pattern, teaches you all the time and keeps reminding you about how to act and react towards things and occurrences' in life!"

Ernest Agyemang Yeboah (Author and teacher)

The writing style you use may not be about the content of the strategy, but it can be vitally important because you want your audience to read the paper. If it's appallingly written, or even just sloppily, you will get the wrong kind of response: the reader will focus on the style, not the substance. More interestingly, writing in an engaging style could bring your audience to agreement and buy-in more quickly and easily.

Just because you are writing a formal paper doesn't mean you suddenly have to write in 'officialese'. You want people to read it, so make it easy to read and understand. A few key points to note:

- Eliminate spelling mistakes and grammatical solecisms.

- Try to avoid clichés. Expressions such as 'transformation' and especially 'digital transformation' have been so overused that they have become almost meaningless. It's not that the concepts are unimportant; you just need to find a different way to make the point. Whenever I find the words 'agile' and 'digital transformation' in a strategy, I am immediately suspicious that they are being used to cover up a lack of thinking and insight.

- Avoid jargon where possible. Only use technical terminology where it is essential to understand the strategy and give a summary explanation if your audience may need it.

- Don't assume everyone understands the acronyms you use. The first time you use an acronym, write it in full, like this: 'Three Letter Acronym (TLA)', and then you can use 'TLA' in the rest of the document. If necessary, include a glossary of terms as part of the backup information. It may well help your readers.

- Use diagrams, graphs or pictures where it makes sense. Not everyone grasps the meaning of things in the same way. Some find a graph indecipherable; others heave a sigh of relief when they see one; consider both types of reader.

- When using PowerPoint, my personal preference is to put a title on each page that explains the content of that page, even if you don't read the rest of it. Sometimes, a summary or conclusions at the bottom of the page is needed. If you take the titles of all the PowerPoint pages, then that should be your short summary of the strategy. It's a good test to see if the paper tells the right story in the right order.

- Use short, simple words. Avoid 'clever' words like 'solecism' (in the first of these points). It may be precisely the right word, but you won't make friends if people need the dictionary to read your paper or because it makes them feel patronised. I apologise for its use earlier, despite retaining it to allow me to make this point.

Consider that your strategy should tell a story. A story is the best way to explain anything: we are all hardwired to relate to stories. It doesn't have to literally be a story, but your explanation of the strategy should progress logically, step by step. If you have an essential part of the case you are making that doesn't fit neatly into the flow, consider: is it really essential? Should it be in the backup information? Why is it there? Could it be somewhere else in the paper? Think about the way that the story fits together. Don't have a series of disconnected charts/paragraphs. If nothing else, there should be a flow, where it is obvious why each chart/paragraph follows on from the previous one.

Even if most strategies aren't really stories, using a real customer history can transform the way that your audience thinks about what you have written. Perhaps a narrative about the customer/ service user experience from today, and then tell the tale of what that experience will be once the strategy is implemented.

Should you write in a formal or informal manner? You should know what your audience expects. If it's formal, that doesn't mean boring or uninteresting. You may not want to include light-hearted comments if writing for a more formal audience, but you still want them to sit up and feel gripped by your strategy.

An informal style can work well with the right audience, but don't overdo it. Whatever you do, be consistent. It's no good having sections of a strategy that read like they were cut and pasted from a Whitehall document when the rest of the paper is informal or chatty. That will divert attention from what you are trying to get across.

What medium to use

The medium for a strategy is probably its least important element. As long as it contains the right information, is clear and concise, you can express it in many ways. The two most obvious examples are a Word document or a PowerPoint presentation, but you can write things down on pieces of paper or on flip charts and save the images. It really doesn't matter as long as you know how you will create, revise, update, store and communicate it.

Having said that, as an important and formal document, it probably makes sense to use a medium that is easily distributed and communicated. Make sure that:

- The strategy document is dated.

  - So that you know when it was written and last updated.

- You use version controls.

  - So that you know what update you are working on. When there are multiple people working on revisions, this is really important.

- It is clear whether it is draft or has received approval.

  - So that you know whether it still needs to be revised and approved or if what you are looking at is the 'official' version.

- It is easy to see what has changed from the previous version.
- Once approved, it is 'locked'.

– To prevent unauthorised modifications. The last thing you need is altered versions of the approved document in circulation.

• There are one or more contact points for anyone who wants to request updates or clarification.

• The document has a management system (see 'How often should a strategy be reviewed'?)

Contents of a strategy

This is one of the things about strategy writing that is really difficult to pin down. I will offer a list of suggested contents, but – as with templates – there are so many exceptions to the rule that it may not be helpful. Many of these will have been covered in earlier chapters and should not surprise you.

Let me start with the things that I would look for, and be surprised if I did not find:

• Executive Summary on a page.

– *which is then explained in more detail by the following sections:*

• Strategic analysis (or context) – explain the current situation of the organisation and the internal/external environments that frame the decisions that have to be taken in the strategy.

• Strategic intent – this is the summary of your strategy and is usually seen before the goals when you have created a situational strategy and after the goals when you have built a goal-based strategy.

• Goals – ensure they are SMART. As previously discussed, not too many!

- Strategic actions (3-6):

  - How the goals will be met.

  - Timings.

  - Actions to be taken.

- Resources to be deployed.

- Financials:

  - Investment required.

  - Implications for capital.

  - Impact on revenue.

  - Impact on operating expense.

  - Impact on profit/loss (surplus/deficit).

- Organisational changes required.

- Internal and external communications.

- Risks and dependencies.

- Management system.

Then there are other sections that often appear – for good reason – in a strategy. They won't be found in every paper, though, so I think of them as relevant for some organisations and not for others. For example, a government function doesn't usually employ sales and marketing professionals, so that section is less likely to be found. Similarly, a routes to market design is not going to be helpful for an NHS Trust, although most commercial organisations would be expected to have this. Some additional sections that may be found in a strategy are:

- Implications for, and involvement of, business partners, suppliers, shareholders, customers/users, local communities.

- Competitor analysis, if not already included in the analysis section.

- Routes to market design and plan.

- IT and digital requirement/implications.

- Sales and marketing requirements, including social media plans and brand implications.

- Environmental and sustainability requirements.

Add to this list if your organisational strategy requires it. Don't expand into operational planning items – that comes later.

Ways to represent the strategy

Of course, you can just throw everything at the paper in the sections suggested here, and that will work if done well. There are more sophisticated ways to represent your strategy, particularly that will enable reviewers and stakeholders to see links between your strategic actions. A strategy map can help you here.

Start with your strategic actions. Let's invent four of these to help set the scene. Let's say that these are for a fictional commercial B2B organisation. These are loosely worded. The targets are not important to illustrate how a strategy map works.

1. Build a significant presence in the consumer goods industry (CGI), from very low penetration today.

2. Develop a competitive digital marketing capability.

3. Build a consulting arm to complement our products.

4. Manage expense to allow investment in actions 1-3 above.

Each of these actions will have key components, and these can be represented:

Build presence in CGI in CGI	Hire Salespeople with CGI skills	Run a marketing campaign aimed at CGI	Recruit Business Partners with CGI presence and credibility
Develop digital marketing capability	Hire marketing people with digital skills	Buy latest digital marketing software suite	Refocus existing marketing budget on digital
Build consulting arm	Hire or aquire capability	Integrate consulting into sales processes	

Manage expense	Fund investment in CGI and new consulting arm	Rebalance marketing budgets towards digital, increase overall by 3% pa	Reduce attrition and hiring costs by 5% pa for 5 years	Reduce admin overhead by 7% pa for next 5 years

Figure 18. A strategy map.

And then you can start to show the relationships between some of these actions:

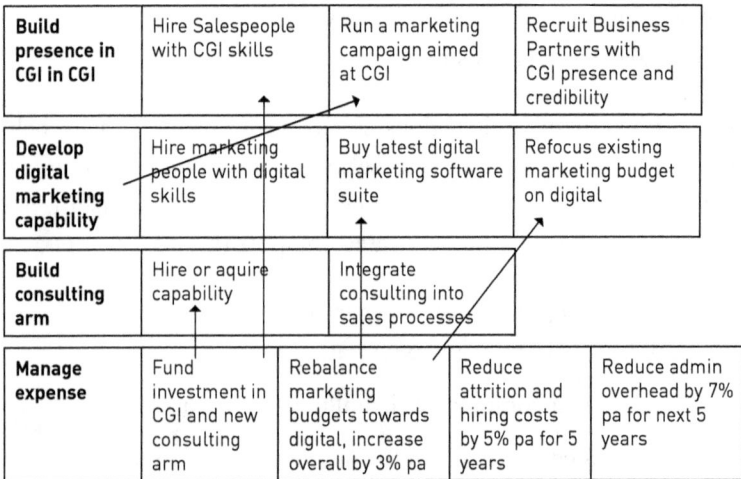

Build presence in CGI in CGI	Hire Salespeople with CGI skills	Run a marketing campaign aimed at CGI	Recruit Business Partners with CGI presence and credibility
Develop digital marketing capability	Hire marketing people with digital skills	Buy latest digital marketing software suite	Refocus existing marketing budget on digital
Build consulting arm	Hire or aquire capability	Integrate consulting into sales processes	

Manage expense	Fund investment in CGI and new consulting arm	Rebalance marketing budgets towards digital, increase overall by 3% pa	Reduce attrition and hiring costs by 5% pa for 5 years	Reduce admin overhead by 7% pa for next 5 years

Figure 19. A strategy map with linkages.

Now, of course, you can use the map to show progress – a sort of basic scorecard, using red, amber and green (RAG) to show progress. In this diagram, red shows as black, amber as light grey and green as darker grey.

Build presence in CGI in CGI	Hire Salespeople with CGI skills	Run a marketing campaign aimed at CGI	Recruit Business Partners with CGI presence and credibility	
Develop digital marketing capability	Hire marketing people with digital skills	Buy latest digital marketing software suite	Refocus existing marketing budget on digital	
Build consulting arm	Hire or acquire capability	Integrate consulting into sales processes		
Manage expense	Fund investment in CGI and new consulting arm	Rebalance marketing budgets towards digital, increase overall by 3% pa	Reduce attrition and hiring costs by 5% pa for 5 years	Reduce admin overhead by 7% pa for next 5 years

Figure 20. A strategy map used as a scorecard.

Lastly, on a more general note, everything – and I mean *everything* – that is in your paper should be there for a reason. There should be no padding, superfluous commentary or irrelevant data. If you are cutting and pasting large chunks of text into the strategy, think long and hard about whether what you are putting in is adding any value. Edit hard and reword where necessary to make the style consistent.

If you can't explain to your boss why something is included, take it out. If you are the boss, then be ruthlessly honest with yourself. Use Albert Einstein's maxim to determine the content: "Everything should be made as simple as possible, but not simpler."

Conclusions:

The tool you use to write your strategy is not important as long as it allows you the required flexibility to manage it through the creation and revision process. Keep it short and use a writing style that fits the audience(s) reading it. Avoid jargon; use graphs and diagrams wherever it will help. Lay it out in a consistent narrative and if it helps to create a strategy map, use that too.

Tests for your strategy:

- Have you got a one page summary that you are happy with?

- Is the style consistent?

- Are you telling a story, or have you got a lot of disconnected pages?

- Have you eliminated jargon and unexplained acronyms?

- Does the appendix contain the information needed to understand the main body?

- Can you manage the distribution, approval, version control and revision processes?

CHAPTER 8

It's written – What Now?

"A plan is not putting you in a box and forcing you to stay there. A plan is a guide to keep you on course, efficient, and safe."

Amber Hurdle (Entrepreneur and author)

OK – so now it's written down in full, and you are clutching the complete draft paper in your hands, or more likely, it's on the H drive of your system. What next? There are quite a few things that you need to do now.

In this chapter, we'll look at what you need to do to turn your draft strategy into something that is being executed in the organisation, has the appropriate reviews and is kept up to date.

Management System

> "However beautiful the strategy, you should
> occasionally look at the results."

Sir Winston Churchill (Statesman)

The first thing we need for your strategy is a system to manage it. Before it goes for approval, you should be able to explain what is being put in place to manage it from draft to execution and keep a cycle of revisions and execution going.

As we saw previously, anyone approving the strategy will need reassurance on three very fundamental questions:

1. *Is this the right thing to do?*
2. *Can it be executed?*
3. *Will it be executed?*

We've already looked at questions one and two in Chapter 6 on strategic actions. The management system is how the third question should be answered. It should explain, simply:

- The measurements that will be used to determine progress and success.
- How progress will be monitored, how often and by whom?
- What constitutes a serious problem, and how it will be handled?
- How often the strategy will be reviewed to make sure it is still valid?
- Approvals required for changes to the strategy (major/minor).

Measurements:

If you have set SMART goals, we know they will be measurable. This is where you define how exactly this happens. Let's look at a simple example. Supposing one of your strategic goals is to attract new customers. Sounds easy to measure, doesn't it? But what counts as a new customer? There's a pure way to do this, which is to count only customers who have never bought from you before. But let's suppose you are selling to the UK government. If you have a sale to Her Majesty's Revenue and Customs (HMRC), who have never bought from you before, that sounds like a new customer; but you may already have sold the same product or service to the Ministry of Defence (MOD). Is HMRC a new customer or not?

When you check your sales records, it turns out that you sold a small deal to HMRC three years ago. Maybe they aren't a new customer after all. But what if that small deal was sold five years ago – or eight? Or twelve? You have to decide on a cut-off. Let's set an arbitrary cut-off of five years and allow the assumption that your small deal was six years ago, so by that definition, HMRC is a new customer. But they remind you that they did a deal last year with another division from your company. Does that make them a new customer for your company or just your division? Assuming the latter, then the company strategy to sell to new customers has not been helped by your sale. At a different level, it may be that your divisional strategy is to find new customers for its product x. If you sold them a large deal three years ago of product y, is this a new customer?

You can see with this simple example that it matters greatly how you define a new customer. The message is: be precise about all the definitions you use when measuring your goals. This is going to be very important when senior managers start to claim victory against the targets; you can be sure that they will interpret the goals in a way that allows them to show themselves in a good light. Tie down the definitions to minimise wriggle room.

You also need to say where the data for these measures will come from. It must be a trusted source, with a *single version of the truth*. Although that sounds both easy and obvious, if you have worked in a large organisation, you will know how hard it is to pin down a single reliable source of data that everyone agrees is the right version. Again, time spent here will be repaid many times over by reducing or eliminating squabbles further down the line.

How progress will be monitored, how often, and by whom: once you have strategic goals defined, these become of great interest to senior people, and by extension, those who work for them. The board will want to see these figures, probably every time they meet. Your executive team need to know what progress is being made in between board meetings. However, they won't just be interested to see the progress towards the ultimate goals in the strategy, which may be as much as five years out. They will expect intermediate targets, 'milestones', to be produced, which plot a course from start to finish of how the measurements should move inexorably towards success.

Let's look at an example of milestones. Again, it's a sales environment, with a strategic goal of creating a new revenue stream of £100m by the end of 2025. Here's a graph showing how your strategy has set the expected yearly achievements:

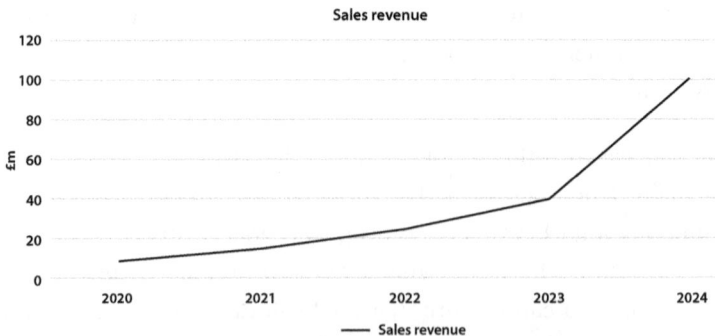

Figure 21. Version one of the milestones for a strategic revenue plan.

Looks healthy and logical, doesn't it? Starting with sales of £10m this year, growing rapidly to £15m in year 2, £25m in year 3, £40m in year 4 and with things in full swing by year 5, £100m by the end of the strategic period. The thinking behind this is that you need to establish a market for your new offering, recruit and train sellers, build a route to market via a network of distributors and retailers, possibly an Original Equipment Manufacturer (OEM) channel, all of which takes time. Let's look at the expected growth percentages and incremental revenue, though.

Year 1: N/A, +£10m

Year 2: 50%, +£5m

Year 3: 66%, +£10m

Year 4: 60%, +£15m

Year 5: 250%, +£60m

The problem is that this is a classic piece of leaving the hard work to the end when people's roles have changed and no one can remember who set up the original targets; not to mention that you will almost certainly have seen huge competition in the market by year five, making it tougher to win revenue. It's crafted to keep the revenue increases possible for the first four years, and then – a miracle occurs. Let's look at a more realistic plan to get to the £100m.

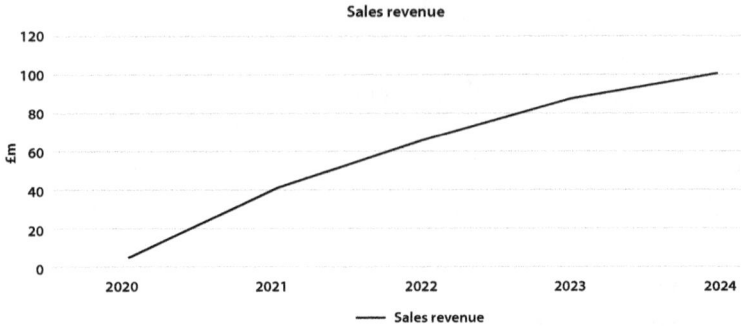

Sales revenue

Figure 22. Version two of the milestones for a strategic revenue plan.

Starting with more realistic sales of £5m this year, with the big hike in growth in year two to £40, £65m in year three, £85m in year four and more modest growth by year five, £100m by the end of the strategic period.

The thinking behind this second version is that you need to move much faster to take the necessary actions to meet your goal. These all have to be accomplished quickly to reap the rewards. Let's look at the expected growth percentages and incremental revenue for this version.

Year 1: N/A, +£5m

Year 2: 700%, +£35m

Year 3: 63%, +£25m

Year 4: 31%, +£20m

Year 5: 18%, +£15m

This time it takes a huge effort – and significant investment – but puts the weight on year two. If things go wrong, there is still time to revise the plan and recover, unlike version one. Make no mistake, getting 18% growth in year five is still going to be a challenge, but nothing like the problems of achieving growth of 250% on revenue of £40m.

Monitoring progress:

Assessing the strategy against its milestones is not the same as the operational management system, with its – possibly – daily reviews of sales figures, revenue, service usage, complaints, social media engagement etc. This is the normal running of the business. It happens with or without a strategy. Looking at the progress of the strategy is on a much less frequent basis. You know it's no good watching a kettle boil – similarly, inspecting the strategic goals too often won't tell you anything and may lead to knee-jerk and thoughtless actions that do more damage than good.

Let's suppose you have a 3-year strategy to turn the business around. The board meets monthly. While the board will look at the key business metrics each time it meets, a review of progress on the strategy might be held every three meetings – or maybe every four. In other words, three or four times a year. If things are working reasonably well, then that's going to be sufficient.

For example, your management system for monitoring progress might state that the strategy will be reviewed by the board in February, May, August and November each year, and 2 hours of the meeting will be devoted to this topic.

What constitutes a serious problem and how it will be handled:

The most obvious approach is to say that deviations from the planned milestones of more than a certain amount will mean a board review earlier than that if the executive team approve it. If it's a relatively small departure from the plan, that's fine – nothing *ever* runs exactly as you planned it. The executives may be comfortable that even a significant shortfall in one area is not a major cause for concern and is fixable. Here's where statistical process control (SPC) can be very helpful. This tells you when natural variation accounts for changes from the average and when the changes are likely to be because something has really changed. Here's a very simple SPC chart:

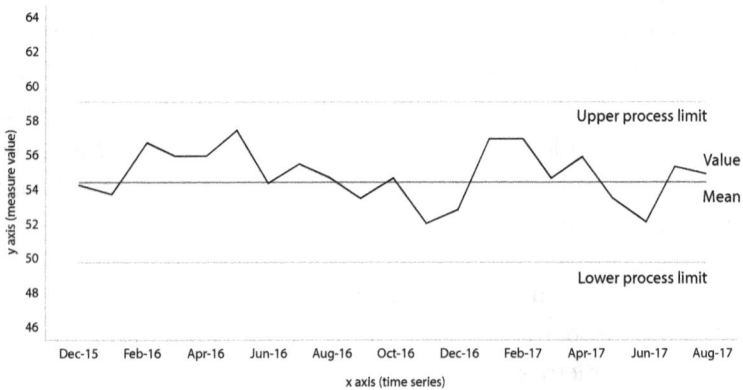

Figure 23. A statistical process control chart. ©NHS 2020. This information is licensed under the Open Government Licence v3.0. To view this licence, visit http://www.nationalarchives.gov.uk/doc/open-government-licence/

The chart shows the varying monthly figures between December 2015 and August 2017. There are enough pieces of data for the process limits to be calculated. The calculation means that 99% of the time, the data will fall between the upper and lower limit. In other words, it's very unlikely that it will go outside the range without a change to the process. So if you see a figure outside that range, you can be confident that it's worth investigating. Looking at the data, you can see that between May 2016 and November 2016, there was a downwards trend to the data, which might trigger all kinds of reviews and action plans. However, we can see that the data stayed well within the limits and the apparent deterioration in results was no more than the normal ups and downs of the process.

However, let's add a target into that picture:

**Figure 24. A statistical process control chart with target.
©NHS 2020. This information is licensed under the Open
Government Licence v3.0. To view this licence, visit
http://www.nationalarchives.gov.uk/doc/open-government-licence/**

With exactly the same data here, we can see that this process is never going to achieve the target without making some changes. The process is consistently failing to meet the target of 62, and with an upper process limit of about 60, there is a vanishingly small likelihood of delivering 62 in any one month, never mind consistently. You absolutely need to take some action to meet the target.

SPC is a complex topic with much more value than the short summary I have given here. It is one tool to ensure that the monitoring process doesn't ring alarm bells unnecessarily, but it does call out processes that are failing.

The discipline of proper data analysis is really important to both operational and strategic understanding. You should only be bringing a serious deviation from the strategic milestones if the data completely supports it. The last thing you want is the board arguing about whether there is a problem or not.

The strategy review cycle

A strategy needs regular reviews to check that it is still fit for purpose (i.e. to meet the defined goals). It is no good faithfully pursuing a strategy that is no longer aligned to your circumstances, environment or goals. It's also folly to keep chasing targets that are obviously not going to be met. This is going to be an area that requires a very open and honest discussion, as there are plenty of ways to get this wrong. Let's take a look first at what a review of the strategy should do. You need to check the first two of the three basic things that we looked at when starting this chapter:

1.   *Is this(still) the right thing to do?*

2.   *Can it (still) be executed?*

The third question, about whether or not it is being executed, we have just discussed as part of the management system. This section takes us back a level and looks at the strategy as a whole. In the words of Constantinos Markides: "Designing a winning strategy is the art of asking questions, experimenting and then constantly renewing the thinking process by questioning the answers. No matter how good today's strategy is, you must always keep reinventing it."

There are several reasons for reviewing the strategy itself:

*   To reflect significant changes in the external environment.

This may be in the form of new legislation/regulation, significant competitive moves or perhaps a new entrant to the market. The first point to make is that the external environment is always changing. If your strategy depended on it staying the same throughout, then you had a poorly designed and inflexible strategy. You should only need to rework your strategy if some unforeseen and significant events affecting your organisation have taken place. Possibly a new government has been elected and introduced new policies or legislation that change the way you have to – or can – operate. This might be a problem or an opportunity. Market deregulation might open up a wealth of new opportunities, or tightening government controls on an element of your business may constrain you in a major way. Either way, you may need to revisit your strategy. Be imaginative – there may be an opportunity in a related industry, there might be a chance to deliver new products or services. You may find a competitor in trouble, or your supply chain may be struggling. It may open up new acquisition opportunities or make a merger a possibility.

- To check that the strategy is capable of delivering the expected milestones and outcomes.

If you can see that your strategy is not going to deliver the expected goals, then you have two options. The first is to change the goals (see next section) or to change the strategy. The latter option is almost always going to be far better because if you set the right goals in the first place, you should not give up on them. The work needed to revise the strategy here is very similar to that discussed in the previous chapter: you have to make decisions about using the resources available to you and whether you need more of them (time, people, budget).

- To examine whether the goals are still valid.

It may be essential to change the strategy's goals – but that should be because the environment has changed, and the goals are no longer appropriate. It could be that the organisation is no longer capable of implementing any strategy that will deliver the goals. In the absence of a major external change, that is something of a damning indictment. It is possible that the wrong goals were set in the first place because the leadership team did not realise what they were signing up to. That's even worse.

A more subtle variation of this review is to change the milestones on the way to the (unaltered) strategic goals. Unless this involves bringing the milestones in earlier, it runs the risk of pushing a known problem out – effectively burying the issue for some time. This is where you should test to make sure that there are really good reasons for changing the milestones.

Approvals required for changes to the strategy (major/minor)

Lastly, you need to define who needs to approve changes to the strategy. It's clear that if there are major changes, it needs to be resubmitted for approval to whichever person or group gave it the original approval – usually the board. Obviously, if some text is being updated to provide additional clarity or some typos are being fixed, then that needs a nod through, and you need to designate who can give that approval. Remember too to keep a log of changes to the paper so that anyone can see what has been done since they last looked at it.

The grey area is, naturally, those changes that could be interpreted as major or minor by different people. While you could devise some guidelines for this, unless you are in a very formally run organisation – perhaps government – then good judgement will allow you to work out what approvals are appropriate. Check with the boss, though. If he or she has a different view, it's worth the debate.

The one-line summary of this section is that if you are going to take the time and trouble to write a strategy, **make sure it remains fit for purpose**.

Getting the strategy approved

"Consensus is a worthy goal, but as a decision-making standard, it can be an obstacle to action or a recipe for lowest-common-denominator compromise. A more practical objective is to get everyone involved to buy in to the decision."

Marcia W. Blenko (Consultant and author)

Now that you have a management system set up for the strategy, you'll need to get it approved (and then operational). There aren't going to be any hard and fast rules for getting approvals, but I can offer some suggestions based on the mistakes I have seen.

Partly, approval is about the internal politics of your organisation. The worst possible reaction to your strategy is indifference. If that's the reaction you get, then – unless something unexpected happens – the strategy is dead in the water. It's far better to get outright opposition because that shows people care and declare their hands about what is wrong (and right) with what you have written. This is when you find out whether your sponsor (if it's not yourself) has got the internal clout to support and defend the strategy and ultimately get it accepted and put into practice. A big argument is a healthy sign, partly because everyone gets to say their piece and partly because if you have done a good job on the creation of the strategy, there will be a lot of evidence that shows why you reached the strategic analysis and from there, the strategic intent. If you have been astute in pulling together the evidence, you will have engaged across the organisation and have discussed elements of the research and strategic analysis with those who are putting up the arguments. If there is a powerful stakeholder who hasn't at least been warned about the contents of the strategy in advance, then you have probably created the problem for yourself.

To avoid some of these issues, make sure you understand the approval process. Is this a chat with the chief executive, or a formal board presentation and review? In most large organisations, it will more typically be the latter. While there will be a formal approval process, in every company I have ever seen, there are some people or steps in the process that are more important than others. If this is a really significant decision for the organisation, like any such decision, it will be settled before the formal approval stage. You aren't going to walk into the board room with a presentation that is new to everyone and win everyone over with your compelling mixture of data, logic and a loveable personality. By the time the board sits down in a meeting, everyone should have had a chance to read the strategy, give feedback and get issues resolved.

The chances are that you have a sponsor who asked you to write the strategy or at least agreed with your suggestion that one was needed. First of all, get your sponsor's support for your paper. If it's a divisional or functional strategy, this may be enough for you to go ahead and implement. If not, then the next step is to circulate the paper for the decision-makers (and influencers) to read and comment. Influencers may also be decision-makers. For example, the CFO is almost always an important person to convince. Once he or she is on board, you will usually find that others are more likely to support. Some influencers may not be formal decision-makers. In government, for example, a special advisor (SPAD) may not have formal decision-making authority, but we know that the minister is very unlikely to approve a strategy without agreement from that SPAD.

Some decision-makers may be perfectly happy with being able to read the paper in advance. Others may require a face-to-face meeting in which the whole strategy is subject to detailed scrutiny and debate.

What I have seen too many times is a strategy paper coming straight to a board, sometimes with advance material being a skimpy and ambiguous PowerPoint. One example from an organisation had an important part of the strategy covered on one chart in seven words.

All too often, no attempt has been made to work out in advance who is likely to question the strategy and withhold approval. On the other hand, I have seen – again, far too often – a board nod through a strategy paper without sufficient scrutiny. Every single time this leads to later difficulties because when the strategy comes back to the next board, there is a flurry of objections to the operational elements because no one checked the strategy in the first place. The board is responsible for making sure it has a strategy (or strategies, if we include divisional, functional and area ones) that it has completely understood and agreed.

If the board gets a strategy that it doesn't understand, for which it doesn't realise the implications, on which it is not completely clear, then that is absolutely the fault of the board. However, post-hoc blame is of no use to anyone. You're still in a mess. So don't give anyone the chance to be less than entirely clear on the strategy and what it is that they are approving. Besides, the board won't blame itself for its lack of understanding; it will blame *you* – no matter how unfair that is. So get the approval process right first time!

- Brief each influencer on the content of the strategy before it is presented for formal approval.

- Leave plenty of time for revisions between sharing with approvers and entering the formal approval process.

- Make sure any disagreements between approvers are resolved in good time or highlighted early so the issues can be ironed out.

- If horse-trading is needed between board members, this is much better resolved in advance, rather than conducting negotiations in front of the rest of the board.

The formal approval process should be brief because everyone has read, understood and agreed the strategy before it enters the formal process. Whatever you do, make sure there are no surprises for the influencers or approvers in the approval process.

As the quotation from Marcia Blenko at the start of this chapter points out, consensus may be the wrong standard for approval for your strategy. Consensus means that everyone agrees with the strategy – which is desirable but not essential. What is vital is that the board – or whoever the key stakeholders are – agree that the strategy should be executed. Getting consensus risks watering down the conclusions, recommended actions or even the strategic intent, and that leads to a less effective strategy. It's unlikely that everyone will be happy with every element – but approval needs to be a fairly speedy process. If it takes you several months to write the strategy and several more to get it approved, that's a long delay while the external world moves on. Speed is therefore essential, not at the expense of true agreement to proceed, but certainly as fast as is practicable.

Of course, there will be internal politics about the strategy: some will want to be seen to support the CEO's direction; others will be positioning themselves to look for weaknesses and show how they spotted it early. There is nothing about the politics here that doesn't happen all the time in the organisation. Just make sure, as far as you can, that the politics don't get in the way of building the right strategy and executing it.

Executing the strategy

> "In reality, strategy is actually very straightforward. You pick a general direction and implement like hell."
>
> **Jack Welch (former CEO of GE)**

While this book is to help you write a strategy in an effective and compelling way and is not really about making the strategy happen, it would not be complete without a short section on execution. After all, this was one of my top ten reasons, at the start of this book, for strategies failing.

First of all, the point of writing your strategy is to get something done. I made the point early on that there is no reason for investing all the time and effort on a strategy that stays in a cupboard (or a shared folder, somewhere on your intranet). Unless someone – possibly you – turns it into reality, it's just an academic exercise.

Turning again to Lou Gerstner on this subject:

"...we [IBM] had outstanding business strategies before. I've read them all, and they were remarkably ahead of their time. The problem was, we never fully implemented them. We sat in meetings, nodded our heads in agreement, and then went back to whatever it was we were doing before. So we agreed we needed to change, but we didn't change."

And Gerstner made bets. He made huge bets. He cut the price of the mainframe, which was the most profitable part of the portfolio. He bought Lotus, for $3.2bn, at that time the largest software deal in history. He bet the company on staying together and not breaking it up as the market expected. Not only did he get the strategy right, even more importantly, he made it happen.

W Chan Kim and Renee Mauborgne acknowledge the importance of execution too:

"...it is only when all the members of an organisation are aligned around a strategy and support it, for better or worse, that a company stands apart as a great and consistent executor."

Or, as Alan Barnard and Chris Parker put it:

"A plan is no more than imagination on a page until our actions bring it to life."

I have talked about a management system for the strategy. I've talked about ways to learn from the results as they come in and tune things to work better. I've talked about how and when to revise the strategy or the goals. None of this can happen if you don't get your organisation in motion to do what you have laid out. This is actually the most important part of having a strategy. Writing it and getting it approved – believe it or not – is actually the easy part.

When you do this in the real world, no matter how hard you work at it, the path of your strategy will not be smooth. As the army says: 'No plan ever survives first contact with the enemy'. In just the same way, when your strategy starts to be executed, there will inevitably be problems. Some big, some small. The determination and leadership skills of the senior executives will be tested.

Getting the strategy executed takes a huge amount of energy, consistently applied over a long period. It takes determination and persistence, even in the best of circumstances.

Communicating the approved strategy

"You can have brilliant ideas, but if you can't get
them across, your ideas won't get you anywhere."

Lee Iacocca (former CEO of Chrysler)

This is where the strategy becomes real. As we have seen, it's not going to be shut in a cupboard and forgotten for 11 months. It is going to inform, motivate and enable your organisation to achieve the goals that the strategy is intended to meet.

Before we dive into the detail of 'how' to communicate, let's take a little while to understand the 'why'.

There's a well-known story about John F Kennedy making his first visit to NASA in 1961. While touring the facility, he introduced himself to a janitor who was mopping the floor and asked him what he did at NASA. "I'm helping put a man on the moon!" replied the janitor. At the risk of stating the obvious, the communication plan for this strategy worked and got to the heart of the intent. The janitor shared the purpose of the whole programme and knew what his part was.

Daniel Pink's influential book, *Drive*, shows that there are three main motivators for people:

- Purpose.
- Autonomy.
- Mastery.

It's worth reading this short book to find out more about all three, but for our line of thought, it's purpose I want to focus on.

Pink states: "The most deeply motivated people… hitch their desires to a cause larger than themselves."

Purpose as a motivator, then, is a sense of alignment between the individual's values and the intent of the organisation that he or she works for. The closer the alignment, the stronger the motivational aspects for the individual.

Coming back to the 'why' of communication, it's not about saying there are new targets, markets, processes, organisations etc. – although all these may be part of the strategy. It's about finding a reason for employees to connect with the direction of travel of the organisation and to give them reasons to think about the strategy, what it means for them as well as your organisation, and to enhance their feeling of belonging – that they are working for the right company.

A strategy should not be something that is done to the organisation or is imposed upon it. Key to success is that all staff and stakeholders understand what you are doing and why. Even if they disagree, clarity on the reasoning behind the change can bring respect and motivation to at least try the change. On the other hand, if there's no apparent reason for the change, and/or the strategy appears to bring no benefit – even in the long-term – for employees, then getting their buy-in is going to be difficult. See the earlier case study about IBM where everyone could see that the strategy meant the risks of worse customer service, reduced budgets and increased likelihood of redundancies.

Even better than good communication is to have the employees feel they have been involved in the creation of the strategy and are invested in it. If they have not been involved in the making of the strategy, and they don't feel involved in its execution, then it's harder to make it happen.

If you have a well-communicated strategy, then everyone will know what you are trying to achieve, which is the first and most important point. The next level of communications explains what each division, department, team and individual should be doing to meet that goal.

The communications element of the strategy needs to build in a few key considerations:

Communications launch

Start though by thinking about the launch. How can you deliver the maximum impact for all employees? It may be that you launch the new strategy for your customers or service users, too – this doesn't have to be an internal exercise only. If going external, it's a good idea to make sure your workforce is fully briefed and expecting this change. Otherwise, when you get inbound contacts, you may get exactly the wrong response from the organisation. You need to be careful, though – as soon as you brief the employees, the secret is out of the bag. So careful timing is vital.

If you are managing this for an international audience, this is even more critical. How are you going to cope with different time zones, different languages and different implementation dates (as strategies are often phased in, with the 'home country' as the first to get started)?

This is a long-term effort

Just as your strategy is (probably) going to take 2-3 years to play out, so your communications about it need to keep a steady drumbeat of information being shared with employees, suppliers, customers, stakeholders and local communities, although each constituency may be receiving different perspectives on the strategy. If you think that a flurry of comms activity at the launch of the strategy is going to work, please think again. It will simply look like another initiative from the top ('the same old, same old') and will barely brush the consciousness of your intended audiences. It will look like a management fad – and we've all seen enough of those. No, if people are to take this seriously, then you need to work really hard on the communications. This is about persuading people that the changes you are making are the right ones, are for the benefit of the organisation and that they should willingly accept new targets, processes, markets, technology or other shifts to their working lives. If you aren't seen to take this seriously and spend a lot of time and effort on it, why would you expect your employees to do so?

Keep it simple

In an ideal world, you would talk in-person to every one of your employees to explain exactly what you mean and what you want them to do. Unless you work for such a small organisation that this is possible, you are going to have to rely on others to get your points across, by whatever means. The more complex the messaging, the more likely it will be interpreted differently – and that means misinterpreted. Pick a few key points and ensure that these are made clearly in every communication that is made. The detail can be made available by other means to those with the interest in learning more.

Here's a good example of a communications asset on a single page from Ofgem, the UK energy regulator, about how it plans to provide regulations that get the UK to net zero emissions from energy by 2050:

How we'll decarbonise energy to deliver a net zero future at the lowest cost to consumers

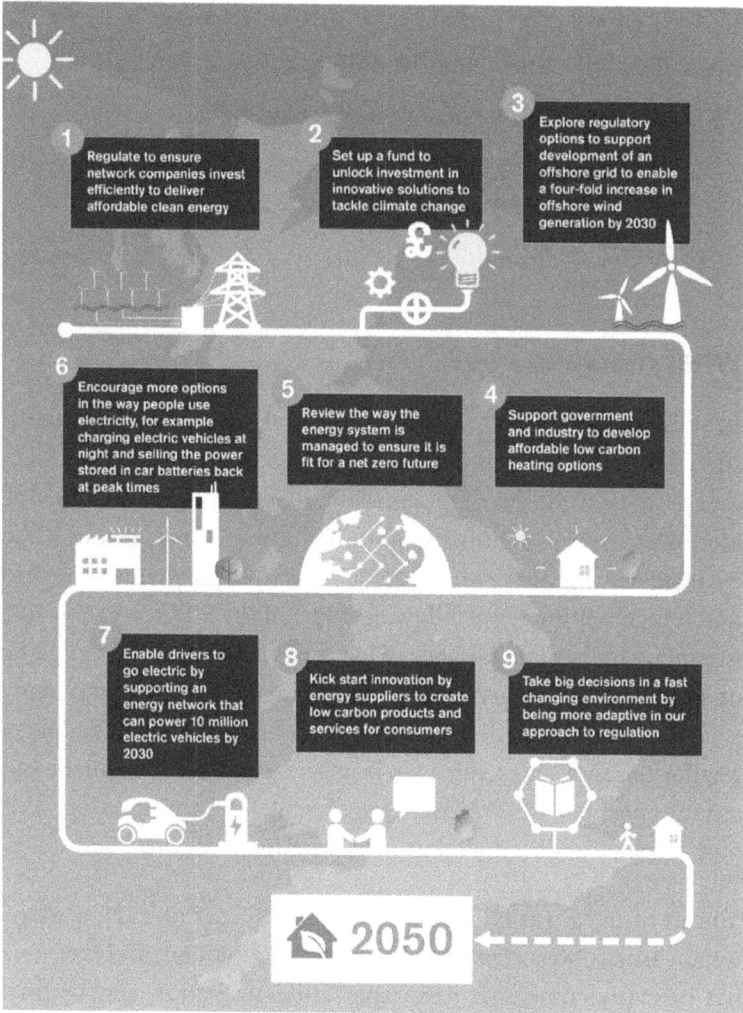

1 Regulate to ensure network companies invest efficiently to deliver affordable clean energy

2 Set up a fund to unlock investment in innovative solutions to tackle climate change

3 Explore regulatory options to support development of an offshore grid to enable a four-fold increase in offshore wind generation by 2030

6 Encourage more options in the way people use electricity, for example charging electric vehicles at night and selling the power stored in car batteries back at peak times

5 Review the way the energy system is managed to ensure it is fit for a net zero future

4 Support government and industry to develop affordable low carbon heating options

7 Enable drivers to go electric by supporting an energy network that can power 10 million electric vehicles by 2030

8 Kick start innovation by energy suppliers to create low carbon products and services for consumers

9 Take big decisions in a fast changing environment by being more adaptive in our approach to regulation

2050

Figure 25. Ofgem's 2050 strategy.
©Ofgem 2020. This information is licensed under the Open Government Licence v3.0. To view this licence, visit http://www.nationalarchives.gov.uk/doc/open-government-licence/

Why I like this way of communicating a strategy:

- It's clear.

- It shows a progression and inter-relationship between the nine different actions/themes.

- It shows when it will have taken effect (2050).

- It works for those who prefer pictorial communication as well as for those who prefer a narrative in words.

- It's on one page.

What media to use?

In most organisations, the CEO will make a video where he or she solemnly explains the situation the organisation faces and tells everyone what the grand plan is. Some employees may even look at it. A proportion of those might watch it all the way through. An even smaller number could possibly take the key points on board and remember them the following day. But the CEO won't be able to explain to them individually what their part in this strategy is; he or she can only give generalisations. This is not to say that making such a video is a bad idea. Exactly the opposite. It's worth making a regular series of short videos to keep the workforce informed, and as far as possible, hear the message directly from the top. But this is only the start and a small part of the communications plan.

You must use a variety of communications methods. Nowadays, we are all used to such a mix of ways to get attention, and everyone has their preferences. For example, I like to read to get the first, second and maybe third level of information. Only when I feel I have that understanding will I be willing to watch a video. Others, on the other hand, would much rather watch a short video to get what they need.

To get a strategy communicated, you should be using all the media you have available, including some unlikely ones. The obvious ones are face to face at 'town hall' meetings (with dozens, if not hundreds) of employees and 'round tables' where the CEO and other senior executives can meet with a smaller number of staff, especially the internal thought leaders. But no CEO of even a moderately sized organisation has time to talk to each person in the company. By briefing managers face to face, you can start to enable them to have informed and positive discussions with their teams and enable them to answer questions and meet objections on the strategy before the issues escalate into rumour, fear, uncertainty and doubt. Done well, this enhances the managers' own positions and drives the communication more accurately and to a deeper level within the organisation than any executive will ever achieve. You'll need to give them the right information and some assets to use when presenting the strategy to their teams.

Next up – email. Everyone seems to think that if you send an email to all employees, you've communicated something. But when you look at how many of these are opened, you would be doing very well indeed to get above 35-40%. And of those, how many click through on the link to your carefully crafted materials? Again, it's a great result to get 10% clicking through… so maybe a maximum of 5% of employees will read the detailed information as a result of your email. You can see this isn't going to be enough. It's *necessary* but not – by a long chalk – *sufficient*. Repeating the email typically gets diminishing results.

If you have a company newsletter, that's a good mechanism for communication, but don't expect too much from it either.

Of the less obvious methods, consider social media – much of which may be visible externally but in practice may be viewed more by employees. Having said that, never lead with social media or allow the employees to think they are learning for the first time through an external platform, something which affects them personally.

Advertising is usually thought of as being for customers or potential customers, but don't forget that your employees will likely see it as well, and they are perhaps more likely to pay attention to the content. It can reinforce a perception that the strategy is real if the external communications are consistent with that strategy, and it shows the organisation is investing (considerable) amounts of money and effort to bring it to life.

Social Proof

In his excellent book on how to influence people, Robert Cialdini talks about the power of social proof.

"...one means we use to determine what is correct is to find out what other people think is correct... We view a behaviour as more correct in a given situation to the degree that we see others performing it."

This means that you need to have advocates for the strategy who have bought into it and are willing persuaders. The obvious candidates are the various layers of management. If they aren't saying the right things, then you are in trouble anyway. So, if managers in your organisation are seen to a) behave consistent with the strategy and b) discuss it and talk about it supportively (the 'think' from the quotation), then that's a good start. Harder to see and harder to obtain is the endorsement of organisational influencers: those who are not in a formal position of authority but are regarded as experts or whose knowledge and experience are such that employees take a cue from their reaction to organisational change. Foot-dragging from this group can undermine people's willingness to make real changes.

I think of the way that people change as like trying to break out of the gravitational pull of the previous way of doing things. It takes a huge amount of energy to get out of the old mindset and processes – but once you have broken free, it's much less likely that people will go back. These influencers need to be part of the energy to break free rather than part of the gravity from previous times.

Use language that means something

I nearly wrote: 'Use authentic language' and then realised that 'authentic' is one of those words that has been so over-used that it has lost much of its meaning. Just like the wording of the strategy itself (see the style section), avoid using cliched words and phrases in your communications. 'World class', 'best of breed', 'agile' are all examples – and there are many more. Find ways to explain what you mean in clear, simple language that isn't lazy.

In summary – the communication of your strategy is incredibly important. It will take time and effort. You will be convinced that you have told everyone too many times and over-communicated, but the reality will be that this is really hard to do, especially if your communications remain engaging and don't cause your audience to switch off. People are generally hungry for good quality, short, clear and consistent information and the more that it a) helps them share in the organisational purpose and b) helps them to do their job, the more it will be valued.

When you are sure that you have told everyone multiple times and you are bored of repeating yourself, the audience might have just started to notice.

Let's look at an interesting case study where communication was built into the strategy:

Case Study: A manufacturing company

Let's take a look at how a manufacturing organisation that had to face a potentially catastrophic situation benefited from creating the right strategy and implementing it. I was lucky enough to be able to interview the former chair (who had recently left to move onto another chair role) and discuss the experience in some detail. I have changed significant details about the company for reasons that will be obvious. I will refer to the chair as Liz – not her real name.

Back in 2013, the newly appointed Liz was assessing this manufacturing company's state. This company supplied complex engineered parts to a variety of manufacturers in several industries and had five manufacturing sites in the UK. It employed about 1,000 people and turned over about £150m pa.

There were pressing financial problems to sort out. Revenue had been fairly stable, but profits were falling fast. The existing executive team knew that a strategy was needed and focused on building one to address the growing financial problems. The new chair agreed that a strategy was needed but not that the focus should be financial, as she regarded those issues as symptomatic rather than fundamental. The key issue to sort out was what was causing the decline in financial performance. At the same time, consultants were appointed to take a root and branch look at the company and deliver a board-level summary of the issues that needed to be addressed.

The consultants' report was duly delivered in March 2014 and proved to be much worse than had been feared. Customer satisfaction was plummeting because of poor relationship management, product quality problems and concerns about the company as a supplier. Employee engagement was weak, with many parts of the organisation coasting, unconcerned about the company's position, and complacent that their own area was 'fine' and doing well. There was a huge disconnect between employee views of performance and customer perceptions. The consultants told of clients who reported a lack of responsiveness, slow product development, poor and inconsistent quality, a lack of attention to detail, as well as delayed and unconvincing responses to complaints. Its once-strong reputation was in tatters within the client base.

It was not all bad. The company was still known – at least historically – for its design and engineering, and there were pockets of excellence, which had played a major part in keeping key clients on board. But these were not the majority of customer engagement experiences. It was also clear that the company was finding it increasingly difficult to attract new customers and was over-reliant on their existing ones.

The financial problems were on a trajectory to get worse, and the consultants expected that several key customers were likely to consider alternative suppliers. Its banks were increasingly reluctant to extend lines of credit. Working capital was drying up.

The consultants' forecast was that the company had 12 months in which to turn itself around. If it continued as it was, beyond that point, the slide would be unstoppable, and it would inevitably face closure or complete restructuring.

In summary, this was a company that was on its knees – financially, reputationally and in terms of customer orders. Doing nothing was not an option.

While the consultants' report was rich in detail, it was obvious to Liz that the rot which had set in was simply because the company had lost sight of its customers. It had become too myopic, too numbers-focused, with little understanding of the vital human asset. It had lost the commitment to serving customers, working with stakeholders and – to put it crudely – the employees thought that the customers were there to keep them all in their jobs.

Taking stock of the root causes, Liz knew that the existing executive team were not up to the job of turning things around. Most had come up through the organisation as engineers, and their leadership experience was limited. They had lost sight of their clients as they changed, and the demands placed upon them gathered pace in their rapidly changing industries. Despite the excoriating nature of the consultants' report, Liz described it as 'brilliant' because it gave the necessary focus and external impetus to drive the changes that were necessary. The only strategy that the company had in place was to address the financial goals, and that was clearly not what was needed.

She took two immediate actions. The first was to replace the CEO, who was not the right person for that role. A good engineer, but not the person the company needed to lead it out of this crisis.

The second was to create a strategy that was fit for purpose. The strategy that had been in place had been imposed from the 'top down' and had failed to engage stakeholders and customers. What was needed was a strategy in whose creation all stakeholders had been involved, were invested in and believed in. The company's customers needed to be at the centre of the design of the strategy. In our terms, the strategic intent was: '**Every** customer will have an outstanding experience of [company name]'. What struck me from talking to Liz was that this wasn't just some management slogan or piece of commercial virtue signalling. She had seen the root cause of the company's problems and was truly passionate about solving the problem by making the customer the centre of the organisational culture.

It took about two months to create the new strategy. That's quick, given the complexity of the business and the extensive nature of the problems that had to be solved. In parallel with that process, Liz and the new CEO recruited an entirely new executive team. This was painful but necessary, as the existing executives didn't have the right skills, experience or attitude to be part of the answer – and there wasn't time to coach them to the point where they could be. The upside, however, was that it gave them the chance to recruit leaders who knew what it was like to work in a leading manufacturing organisation. Each one came with knowledge of how it *felt* to be part of a culture that was customer-focused and successful.

The strategy had to consider whether all five plants could stay open and whether the existing products should be continued. Some products – including ones that had helped this company make its name – had to be discontinued. This caused problems because staff – and a few customers – strongly associated the company with these products and had deep emotional attachments to them. However, when looked at dispassionately, they were not attracting new clients, were losing ground to more impressive competitors and were loss-making. There was no choice. There were also several products with short runs but high staffing levels – those had to be cut.

Harder to judge was whether to keep all five manufacturing facilities open. The purely numbers-based analysis performed by the consultants suggested that one should be closed. After much careful consideration, the leadership team concluded that the offer it could make to customers would be diminished too much by closing the most threatened site. This was more an emotional than a rational decision, but in the long run (at least between 2014 and today) turned out to be the right decision.

The key criterion for this difficult decision was the strategic intent to focus on meeting the customers' needs, and this was made easier by keeping the plant open. Liz refers back to the purpose of the organisation as an important reference point for making this call.

Key to the success of the strategy was communication.

First of all, they went out to the five sites – regularly – to explain what they were doing and why. Their key messages were simple:

- If we keep doing what we've been doing, we will get the same results. We will close.

- We are going to put the customer first in everything that we do, from the smallest to the largest companies we supply.

- Everyone's performance is under scrutiny – from top to bottom because the company's performance is under scrutiny.

- Everyone in the company has to perform, no exceptions. Do well, and you'll get more work and more pay. Fail to meet the performance needed, and we'll ask you to leave.

- Everyone has to buy into the new vision of the company – expressed as: 'You have to be on the bus'. (There was literally a picture of a bus in every presentation to the staff.)

Every site had a face-to-face meeting every month for two years – a significant investment of time and effort from the leadership team, but one they felt was essential to the future of the organisation.

The new leadership team delivered these messages, not just in all-hands meetings on site, but in departmental meetings, 1-1s... in short, at every opportunity. In Liz's words, few of them were natural communicators or presenters, but what was more important was their enthusiasm and commitment. The better employees bought into those qualities and became similarly committed. Many others left – without prompting – because they knew that what they could offer was no longer what was needed.

By now, things had changed but were not yet on track. The strategy needed to be updated in light of the changes to the capabilities of the company. Here's where this organisation did something really quite unusual: they truly involved the employees in the formulation of the updates to the strategy. Workshops were held which involved every employee in each of the sites. These workshops were led by the executive team, but not as a broadcast of what they already knew – they were there to facilitate the expression of employee ideas, suggestions, feedback and reactions. Staff were asked a variety of questions to elicit the right discussion, and their answers to the questions were captured in real-time so that everyone could see how their peers were responding. Through their involvement, the strategy evolved to become even more customer-friendly, and because they had been involved, a virtuous circle was created – whereby the motivated employees were further engaged by the discussions and the knowledge that the leadership team were listening to them and changing the strategy in line with their suggestions.

The revisions to the strategy were possibly less important, suggests Liz, than the fact that the process generated excitement, pride and belief. Everyone was truly 'on the bus'. It's worth noting that the regular discussions with employees did not end once the strategy was revised – they continue to this day.

Now, this sounds easy, but like all real-world strategy work, it was complicated, messy and far from clear at the time. The strategic intent stayed constant and underpinned the work throughout, and that is what kept them on track.

I asked Liz whether there were tough decisions and trade-offs to be made. "Of course. We had to lose staff – and risk our production capacity. As it turned out, we got through the work OK, but not without some close calls." She thought about the difficult choices forced on them by their strategy. "We had to take a decision about a flagship product line. In the end, it was clear that we couldn't sustain it profitably, but that generated a lot of emotion, as it was interwoven with the company history. By pruning hard, we saved the whole company – but it was never easy."

So where are they now? The company achieved its self-imposed 12-month deadline to turn the business around. They have still got all five plants open and are operating profitably. Cash flow is easing, and the banks are happier to discuss lines of credit. More importantly, customer satisfaction – measured in many more ways than before – is way up, and they are finding it much easier to find customers who will provide testimonials to help create marketing assets. There is a steady inflow of new clients – still hard to win, but now possible. There is still much to work on, but they know they had the right strategy.

Learnings:

What is noticeable was the swift and confident strategic analysis, getting the strategic intent right and putting the right strategic actions in place. Having a strong and effective leadership team was vital to this, and much of the executive team was replaced.

Success came because of employee involvement in strategy creation and updates and getting the right strategic intent. It should go without saying that every company or organisation should be customer-focused. It doesn't necessarily mean that this is the right strategic intent to for your strategy to pursue – that will depend on your own circumstances – as long as you don't lose sight of the client or service user. Any organisation that doesn't have the customer/service user at the heart of its culture will not succeed in the long-term, no matter what.

The communication plan for the strategy was an integral part of the execution. Managers and executives reinforced key points, explained progress, invited comments and worked with employees to refine the strategy. They got the buy-in needed to save the company.

Conclusions:

In this chapter we started with your draft strategy. You've ensured that it has a management system defined for it; you've been through the approvals process, and it has had formal approval; you've built your communications plan.

Now all you have to do is make it happen! And that's where the action happens. Everything you have spent such a long time thinking about and planning is now going to meet the real world. Don't worry that your strategy isn't perfect. The perfect strategy has yet to be written. The important thing is that it takes your organisation in the right direction, at the right speed and in the right way, helping it to become better and more effective at what it does. For some of you, survival will be the measure of success. For others, perhaps you have set out on a path of dominance in your market sector. For a very few (and I really mean a very few), you will truly achieve world-class status. Whatever your kind of organisation and whatever your path forward, I hope that this has been a helpful guide to negotiating the journey involved in writing a strategy. Now you are ready to start all over again!

Tests for your Strategy:

- Is your management system defined?

- Does it make clear how measurements are defined?

- Do you have sufficiently ambitious milestones?

- Do you know how you will monitor progress?

- When and how will strategy reviews take place?

- How will your strategy receive approval?

- Will it ever be executed?

- Do you have a comprehensive communication plan for your strategy?

CHAPTER 9

Over to You

"Strategy is about stretching limited resources to fit ambitious aspirations."

C. K. Prahalad
(Professor of Corporate Strategy at University of Michigan)

Now it's time for you to take what you have learned and apply it to your own organisation.

Let's always remember that writing a strategy is actually the easiest part of strategy. As the management guru, Peter Drucker, says: "Strategy is a commodity, execution is an art." Bill Gates, of Microsoft fame, put it like this: "A bad strategy will fail no matter how good your information is, and lame execution will stymie a good strategy. If you do enough things poorly, you will go out of business."

I hope that by reading this book, you will avoid the mistakes that I have made when trying to write strategies and the ones that I see regularly every working day.

If there's one last piece of advice for me to give, it is this: facts are your friends. When thinking about, building, getting approval for and communicating your strategy, the better the understanding you have of the organisation, the environment (current and predicted), the competition, and your goals, the better the results will be. Facts will enable you to convince stakeholders; facts will enable you to get the best possible strategic analysis; they will provide examples that will illuminate your communications and will enable you to check how the strategy is working in the real world. Avoid opinion, anecdote and guesswork. They will simply make your life harder.

If you are lucky enough to be able to combine inspiration with facts and hard work, the chances are that you will have a great strategy. Thomas Edison is credited with saying that genius is 1% inspiration and 99% perspiration. We can all do the hard work, even if only a few can do the flashes of genius. Writing a good strategy isn't about being the next Steve Jobs or Jack Welch. It's about making your organisation sustainably successful.

I wish you the best of luck – and plenty of hard work that should make luck redundant.

BIBLIOGRAPHY

All these books have informed my thinking in writing this book, to a greater or lesser extent. They are listed alphabetically, by author.

Campaign It! Alan Barnard and Chris Parker

Blue Ocean Strategy. W Chan Kim and Renee Mauborgne

Influence: The Psychology of Persuasion. Robert Cialdini

On The Psychology of Military Incompetence. Norman Dixon

Who Says Elephants Can't Dance? Lou Gerstner

How to Think. Alan Jacobs

Thinking, Fast and Slow. Daniel Kahneman

The Strategist: Be The Leader Your Business Needs. Cynthia A Montgomery

Inside The Tornado. Geoffrey A Moore

The Power of Purpose. John O'Brien and Andrew Cave

Drive. Daniel H Pink

Competitive Strategy. Michael Porter

Good Strategy/Bad Strategy. Richard Rumelt

Social Media Strategy. Martin Thomas

The End Of Marketing As We Know It. Sergio Zyman

ABOUT THE AUTHOR

Michael is a Non-Executive Director, Board Advisor, Trustee, Consultant and School Governor. He worked for IBM for more than 30 years before concentrating on strategy. For several years, he wrote IBM UK's marketing strategy, before taking responsibility for creating the hardware marketing strategy for Europe.

Michael sits on the boards of an NHS Trust, a fast-growing social enterprise, two charities, a leading school and on the Advisory Board at Exeter Business School, where he regularly reviews strategies and contributes to their creation. He has set up a strategy consultancy, House Of Strategy, with a colleague.

He lives in Wiltshire, is married with three children and spends what spare time he has playing guitar and golf.

Contact via houseofstrategy.co.uk

REFERENCES

1   *"Toyota 75 year history, Part 3. Leaping Forward as a Global Organisation"*, accessed July 14th, 2021, http://www.toyota-global.com/company/history_of_toyota/75years/text/leaping_forward_as_a_global_corporation/index.html

2   Steve Denning, *"Why IBM Is In Decline"*, *Forbes*, May 30th, 2014, https://www.forbes.com/sites/stevedenning/2014/05/30/why-ibm-is-in-decline/#4736d17b3e48

3   *"The Brain of an F1 Car"*, February 7th, 2018, https://www.mclaren.com/applied/lab/brain-of-an-f1-car-mclaren-ecu/

4   Michael Hiltzik, *"Kodak's long fade to black"*, *Los Angeles Times*, December 4th, 2011, https://www.latimes.com/business/la-xpm-2011-dec-04-la-fi-hiltzik-20111204-story.html

5   Jeremy Miller, *"6 Inspiring Vision Statements that Built Iconic Brands"*, April 26th, 2016,

https://stickybranding.com/6-inspiring-vision-statements-that-built-iconic-brands/

6   Kotter, *"Barriers to Change: The Real Reason Behind the Kodak Downfall"*, May 2nd, 2012,

https://www.forbes.com/sites/johnkotter/2012/05/02/barriers-to-change-the-real-reason-behind-the-kodak-downfall/

7   *"BMW Group Strategy"*, accessed July 14th, 2021, https://www.bmwgroup.com/en/company/strategie.html

8   *"Tesla Battery Day Presentation Pack"*, September 22nd, 2020, https://tesla-share.thron.com/content/?id=96ea71cf-8fda-4648-a62c-753af436c3b6&pkey=S1dbei4

9   *"Rule Book 2019"*, accessed July 14th, 2021, https://labour.
org.uk/wp-content/uploads/2019/04/Rule-Book-2019.pdf

10   *"Working At Amazon"*, accessed July 14th, 2021, https://
amazon.jobs/en-gb/working/working-amazon

11   *"BMW Group Strategy"*, accessed 14th Jul, 2021, https://
www.bmwgroup.com/en/company/strategie.html

12   *"Vision & Business Idea"*, accessed July 14th, 2021, https://
www.ikea.com/gb/en/this-is-ikea/about-us/vision-and-business-
idea-pub9cd02291

13   *"Plans, Reports and Policies"*, accessed July 14th, 2021,
https://www.oxfam.org.uk/what-we-do/about-us/plans-reports-
and-policies

14   *"ONE COMPANY, ONE VISION: TO CREATE
INNOVATIONS."*, accessed July 14th, 2021,

https://www.bmwgroup.com/en/innovation/company.html

15   *"Vision & Business Idea"*, accessed July 14th, 2021, https://
www.ikea.com/gb/en/this-is-ikea/about-us/vision-and-business-
idea-pub9cd02291

16   *"Leadership Principles"*, accessed July 14th, 2021, https://
www.amazon.jobs/en-gb/principles

17   *"2015 Corporate Responsibility Report. Our approach to corporate
responsibility"*, accessed July 14th, 2021, https://www.ibm.com/
ibm/responsibility/2015/at_a_glance/our_approach.html

18   *"The Trust"*, accessed July 14th, 2021, https://www.
southernhealth.nhs.uk/about-us/trust

19   *"Purpose, values & principles"*, accessed July 14th, 2021,

https://www.unilever.co.uk/about/who-we-are/purpose-and-principles/

20   *"Policies and Practices"*, accessed July 14th, 2021, https://us.pg.com/policies-and-practices/purpose-values-and-principles/

21   *"Purpose, values & principles"*, accessed July 14th, 2021, https://www.unilever.co.uk/about/who-we-are/purpose-and-principles/

22   Marty Swant, *"The World's 20 Most Valuable Brands"*, accessed July 14th, 2021, https://www.forbes.com/powerful-brands/list/#tab:rank

23   *"Our Strategy"*, accessed January 17th, 2021, http://investor.harley-davidson.com/our-company/our-strategy

24   *"What is corporate governance?"*, accessed July 14th, 2021, https://www.icsa.org.uk/about-us/policy/what-is-corporate-governance

25   *"Technology Investment Roadmap Discussion Paper"*, May 2020, https://consult.industry.gov.au/climate-change/technology-investment-roadmap/supporting_documents/technologyinvestmentroadmapdiscussionpaper.pdf

26   *"Sustainable Development Report 2021"*, June 14th, 2021,

https://www.sustainabledevelopment.report/reports/sustainable-development-report-2021/

27   *"Nokia net sales worldwide from 1999 to 2020"*, accessed July 14th, 2021,

https://www.statista.com/statistics/267819/nokias-net-sales-since-1999/

28   *"Historical components of the Dow Jones Industrial Average"*, August 31st, 2020,

https://en.wikipedia.org/wiki/Historical_components_of_the_Dow_Jones_Industrial_Average

29   *"FTSE 100 History"*, accessed July 14th, 2021, https://www.ig.com/uk/indices/markets-indices/ftse-100/ftse-100-history#information-banner-dismiss

30   *"IBM Highlights, 1970-1984"*, accessed July 14th, 2021, https://www.ibm.com/ibm/history/documents/pdf/1970-1984.pdf

31   *"The IKEA sustainability strategy – making a real difference"*, accessed July 14th, 2021,

https://www.ikea.com/gb/en/this-is-ikea/about-us/the-ikea-sustainability-strategy-making-a-real-difference-pubb5534570

32   *"Our strategy"*, accessed July 14th, 2021, https://www.unilever.com/our-company/strategy/

33   *"2020 Battery Day Presentation Deck"*, September 22nd, 2020, https://tesla-share.thron.com/content/?id=96ea71cf-8fda-4648-a62c-753af436c3b6&pkey=S1dbei4

34   *"Our strategy"*, accessed July 14th, 2021, https://www.hsbc.com/who-we-are/purpose-values-and-strategy/our-strategy